SIMPLE
FARMHOUSE
LIFE

SIMPLE FARMHOUSE LIFE

DIY PROJECTS FOR THE
ALL-NATURAL, HANDMADE HOME

LISA BASS

LYONS PRESS

Guilford, Connecticut

*Dedicated to my husband, Luke, who kept the kids busy while
I wrote and photographed every single project in this book.
Also, to my blog readers and YouTube followers, who
push me daily to keep creating!*

An imprint of The Rowman & Littlefield Publishing Group, Inc.
4501 Forbes Blvd., Ste. 200
Lanham, MD 20706
www.rowman.com

Distributed by NATIONAL BOOK NETWORK

British Library Cataloguing in Publication Information available

Library of Congress Control Number: 2019950490

ISBN 978-1-4930-4274-6 (paperback)
ISBN 978-1-4930-4275-3 (e-book)

∞™ The paper used in this publication meets the minimum requirements of American National Standard for Information Sciences—
Permanence of Paper for Printed Library Materials, ANSI/NISO Z39.48-1992.

CONTENTS

INTRODUCTION

My name is Lisa, and I am the photographer, videographer, and author behind the blog *Farmhouse on Boone*. I live in a 130-year-old Victorian farmhouse with my husband Luke and our six kids. Though our journey into making this property our dream homestead is just beginning, a simple and slow lifestyle is something I have wanted my whole life, even if I didn't always know it.

I grew up on a farm in the Midwest, where I spent countless hours outside playing with my sisters and cousins, throwing rocks in the creek and counting animals with my dad. We lived on a dreamy 400-acre property complete with a herd of forty elk, my grandpa's cattle, an old silo, and as many outbuildings and barns to explore as any kid could dream of. I had my own pony named Blaze, my beagle, Mami, and way too many barn cats to remember.

Where I'm from, most of my friends grew up in similar ways, so I didn't really know it was special. Climbing eight-foot-tall fences, ducking under barbed wire, and watching my parents pull a calf from a distressed elk cow were all parts of a normal life for this country kid. When my friends came over in middle school, our fun consisted of racing down rows of twenty round hay bales and searching for the kittens from the latest cat we suspected was pregnant.

I tried city life for a few years in college and felt like a fish out of water. It was fun for a time, but something about it just never felt like home. Driving down city streets couldn't compare to rows of knotty fence posts, the smell of cows, and driving past acres of cornfields. I knew where I would eventually end up.

I graduated college in 2007 and married later that year. With a baby on the way soon afterward, I traded in career goals for a life at home with my little girl. It was there I rediscovered my passion for creative and simple living. I remember struggling through my first sewing pattern since my elementary school 4-H years, while my mom helped me decipher the meaning of *selvage* and *baste stitch*. I played around with different colors and patterns of cotton fabric to make ruffled bloomers and dresses for my daughter. I tried my hand at bread baking and milling whole grains. I learned how to cook with cast iron and make hand-poured candles. Good, old-fashioned homemaking inspired me, and I wanted to learn absolutely everything I could.

Digging into some influential books and online research led me to the wonderful world of raw milk, fermented vegetables, traditional sourdough bread making, and homesteading. I learned how to make basic products for our home and bodies with natural ingredients and essential oils.

I started dreaming of gravel roads, backyard chickens, and a couple of goats to milk. The simple lifestyle beckoned. At the time, we didn't have a whole lot of space to work with on our lot in

our small hometown, but we filled what we did have with five laying hens and a garden that took up most of our backyard. We searched high and low for a larger lot to move our growing family to, but with a commitment to living within our means and freedom from debt, the timing just never felt quite right. Though certain animals weren't allowed in town, I almost had Luke talked into hiding a couple of dairy goats just behind the playset in our yard. We may not have had our true farmhouse and land yet, but I wasn't going to be deterred from living the lifestyle.

In December 2015 I started my blog, where I share my handmade project ideas, from-scratch recipes, and natural DIYs with other dreamers who desire to learn those old-fashioned skills. A couple of years later, in 2017, I began creating simple-living videos for my *Farmhouse on Boone* YouTube channel. In 2018, Luke quit his job of over thirteen years to come home and pursue our online business together. As my online presence rapidly grew, it became very apparent to me that simple living is a craving shared by many people today.

People want to know what they're putting on and in their bodies; they want to feel more connected with the origins of basic things. As we get further removed from our handmade roots, we want to enjoy those simple pleasures of life that our grandparents knew. While life was very difficult back then, nowadays we get to enjoy modern conveniences and still have the leisure time to pursue handcrafting and from-scratch living, while our washing machines toil away in the other room. There has never been a better time in history to be alive. I am so truly blessed to share creative content full-time for a living, with my family by my side.

After making our home in a Craftsman bungalow on a quarter-acre in town for the first ten years of our marriage, Luke and I recently closed on a seven-acre plot complete with an old white barn, two tiny cottages, and a turn-of-the-century brick silo. With six kids in tow, and three of them rambunctious boys, the timing was finally right. We had saved up enough money to purchase this property, where our kids can enjoy the same country life that I had growing up. There are trees to climb, barn stalls for future horses, and plenty of dirt for worm and roly poly collecting. The opportunity to transform the interior of our farmhouse and turn our small plot of land into a functioning homestead is a dream come true. I am looking forward to sewing heaps of curtains, pillows, and slipcovers, selecting the perfect antiques, and putting my own personal homespun stamp on every inch of this place.

We aren't quite on a gravel road, but finally we will have the space to get the goats and fruit trees I have always dreamed of. Though I've spent years learning how to make things with my own two hands and trying to master the basics of running a diverse, small-scale hobby farm, our

story with this property is just beginning. I want to do it all—milk the cow, gather the eggs, can fruit, and line up homemade pies on the windowsill. For now we are taking it slowly, enjoying the process along the way and learning as we go.

My story has taken many twists and turns over the years, but I am every bit as passionate about creating a handmade home and simple farmhouse life as I've ever been. There is nothing like the satisfaction of seeing something you've dreamt up and made with your own two hands, whether it be a carefully curated flower arrangement in a chipped ironstone pitcher, a simple crocheted baby blanket, a luxurious handcrafted lotion bar, or a beautiful garden with bountiful rows of tomatoes and cucumbers.

I find freedom in a simple and minimal lifestyle. Freedom to live on a little less, to have the time and resources to enjoy the simple things in life a little more. I hope my passion for creativity and handcrafting will inspire you to create a home and lifestyle that you love.

CHAPTER 1

NATURAL HANDMADE KITCHEN

CREATING A BEAUTIFUL, NATURAL KITCHEN doesn't need to be complicated or expensive. In the spirit of simplicity, I like to add seasonal touches with elements straight from the outdoors, such as fresh cedar, eucalyptus, and pinecones in the winter months, Jarrahdale pumpkins in the fall, and bouquets of zinnias and cosmos all summer long.

There is so much beauty in the ordinary and useful, like the vintage scissors that sit out on the counter, or the crock that collects wooden spoons and rolling pins by the stove. Items that can double as something aesthetically pleasing and useful are something I keep a keen eye out for.

As a three-meal-a-day chef for my family of seven, I need space for crocks of sauerkraut and sourdough baked goods. At any given moment, there are three half-gallon Mason jars fermenting milk kefir and homemade pickles. A couple of apron-clad littles often pop in to offer a helping hand kneading bread dough and chopping veggies. Each item in the kitchen needs to be intentional, to keep everything clutter-free and running smoothly.

Linen aprons, cutting boards, skillets, and drying herbs are all proudly displayed as part of the decor and charm. I like to keep my cookware, storage containers, and utensils simple, with a focus on cast iron, stainless steel, wicker, and wood. Essential oils and basic ingredients, like beeswax, castile soap, and coconut oil, allow me to care for my kitchen wares and keep things clean in a natural way.

BEESWAX FOOD WRAPS

Finished dimensions: 12 inches by 12 inches | Yield: 5 wraps

Glass storage containers and a small collection of beeswax wraps are all you need for all-natural food storage. As a reusable alternative to plastic wrap, these wraps are perfect to throw over a plate or bowl that doesn't have a lid. The beeswax on the fabric creates an airtight seal so that the food inside stays fresher, longer.

Use the wraps for sandwiches, blocks of cheese, sliced veggies, and that half-eaten apple your toddler left on his high chair. You can mold the wraps with the heat of your hand to conform around any plate, cup, apple, or carrot stick, and they will hold their shape as they cool.

Wash the wraps in cold water with a mild soap, such as the foaming dish soap on page 30. Never use hot water, as the beeswax will melt and break the airtight seal on the fabric.

MATERIALS

1 yard 100 percent cotton fabric

5 ounces beeswax, grated

CUT

Five 12-by-12-inch squares of fabric

INSTRUCTIONS

Preheat oven to 170 degrees.

Place one square fabric piece on a parchment paper–lined baking sheet. Sprinkle the fabric with grated beeswax. Bake 7 minutes, or until melted.

Spread the melted beeswax around the fabric with a paintbrush to cover any spots that aren't coated yet. The beeswax will stick to the brush and be very difficult to remove, so be sure to use a cheap one that you

don't mind discarding afterward. You can put the paintbrush on the baking sheet, into the oven with the wraps, so the wax doesn't harden on the brush between batches.

Put the baking sheet back in the oven for another couple of minutes to ensure that everything is melted evenly. Immediately remove the wrap from the baking sheet so that the beeswax doesn't harden and stick. This will happen instantly. Hang the wrap on a clothesline for a few minutes, or until the wax has fully hardened.

Repeat until all five fabric pieces are coated with beeswax. These beeswax wraps will last for up to one year.

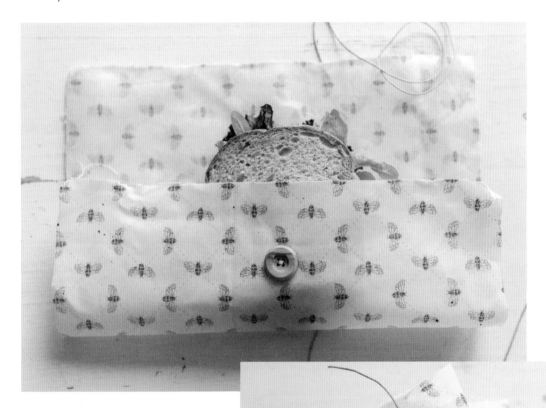

To create airtight sandwich storage, sew a large button near the top center area of one of the wraps. Fold it around the sandwich and secure shut with jute twine.

SIMPLE POT HOLDERS

If you're in your kitchen for three meals a day, like I am, you probably feel like you have an infinite need for pot holders. Somehow my stash of ten dwindles down to two without any warning, and I'm caught stuffing linen tea towels under the four hot pots and pans on the table. If they don't mysteriously disappear, they are filthy dirty and burned beyond what a couple cycles through the washing machine can fix. I used to make quilted pot holders with the pretty coordinating bias-tape edge, but when I noticed how quickly my perfect creations were ruined, I switched over to this more-practical method. Mama only has so much time to spend sewing something that gets burned and gross anyway.

MATERIALS

10-inch fabric scraps (Almost anything goes for this: denim, cotton, linen, grain sack, and drop cloth are all great choices. The only thing I would avoid using is super-lightweight fabrics.)

Insulation material (quilt batting, scrap denim, old dish towels, drop cloth, flannel, or Insul-Bright)

INSTRUCTIONS

Measure, mark, and cut 10-inch squares of fabric (cut two), a 1½-by-4-inch piece for the loop (cut one), 10-inch squares of the insulation material (cut two to three). I have tried several options for insulating my handmade pot holders, from a few layers of denim and old terry washcloths, to several layers of cotton quilt batting. Before you sew the layers together, you can test how protective they will be by stacking them all up and grabbing the handle of a hot cast-iron pan. If you can only pick it up for a few seconds, you may want to rethink the configuration.

If you do a lot of Internet research on how to make pot holders, you will encounter a product called Insul-Brite. Layering one piece of the highly insulating polyester material between two layers of quilt batting seems to be the most surefire way to get a heavily insulated pot holder, although I have never used it myself, and have still made many effective pot holders with items I have laying around the house.

Prepare the loop piece. Fold the 1½-inch-by-4-inch loop piece in half lengthwise, with the right sides together, and sew down the long side with a very narrow seam. Use a safety pin to turn the loop piece right side out. Press the loop piece flat and topstitch along the seam.

Stack your 10-inch pieces of insulation material on your work surface. Layer on top of that the two 10-inch fabric pieces, with right sides together. Fold the loop in half and lay it on one of the corners, with the raw edges facing out, between the two fabric pieces. Pin the layers together.

Sew all the way around the pot holder with a ½-inch seam, leaving a 4-inch opening. Trim the corners, and any excess insulation material, to remove some of the bulk.

Use the 4-inch opening to turn the pot holder right side out, exposing the main fabric and loop, and hiding all of the insulation material inside.

Topstitch all the way around the pot holder with a ¼-inch seam. This will also close the 4-inch area that you left open.

Sew a few lines down the middle to hold the layers together. If you're in a hurry, one line down the center will work just fine. You could also sew all the way across with vertical and horizontal lines to make the pot holder look more quilted; just make sure the lines are evenly spaced.

LINEN TEA TOWELS

Finished dimensions: If the linen is 56 inches wide, this will yield four tea towels, each 27 by 17 inches. If it is 43 inches wide, the finished tea towels will be 20½ inches by 17 inches.

Linen has the natural ability to prevent bacterial growth, making it the perfect choice for tea towels. Because of the loose weave, linen dries more quickly than cotton. This textile is stronger than most others, and is highly absorbent. The linen fabric may seem a little stiff at first, but it will get softer, and more absorbent, with each and every wash. I like to use tea towels in place of terry washcloths because they dry more quickly. They stay fresh-smelling longer and are just as effective in wiping up counters and dishes. They are also great to lay over ferments in the kitchen, like sourdough starter and milk kefir.

I think linen in muted blue, cream, and oatmeal tones is the most beautiful.

MATERIALS

1 yard medium-weight linen (43 to 56 inches wide)

INSTRUCTIONS

Cut the yard of linen in four equal parts.

Press all four sides over ½ inch and then another ½ inch, hiding the raw edges inside.

Sew all the way around with a ⅜-inch hem.

SIMPLE LINEN MARKET TOTE

Finished dimensions: 16½ inches by 15 inches, plus straps approximately 13½ inches

We often need to grab a tote bag as we are leaving the farmhouse with all the kiddos. Whether it's to stuff it full of swimming gear for a dip in the creek, or for a quick trip to the market, we can never have too many bags hanging around, especially when they're pretty! I like to stick to colors that fit in with my home decor, so I don't mind them hanging in the mudroom, waiting to be used. Form plus function wins again.

MATERIALS

1 yard of linen, or linen-blend, fabric

MEASURE AND CUT

**Cut two for the straps,
    4 inches by 28 inches**

**Cut two for the main piece,
    16 inches by 18 inches**

INSTRUCTIONS

Fold one strap piece in half all the way down the long side, right sides together, and sew a ¼-inch seam. Leave the two ends open. Using a large safety pin at one corner, turn the strap right side out. Press the seam flat. Topstitch all along the two long sides with a very narrow seam. Repeat with the other strap piece.

With right sides together, sew the two 16-by-18-inch main pieces together with a ½-inch seam. Finish the raw seams with a serger or zigzag stitch.

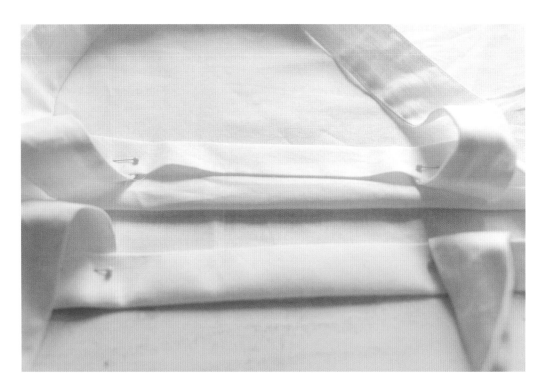

Turn the bag right side out. Fold the top edge of the bag down 1 inch to the inside of the bag, and press in place. Fold it one more time, to hide the raw edges inside, and press in place.

Place the raw edges of the straps underneath the pressed fold at the top of the bag, on the front of the bag. Pin in place. Each edge of the strap should be placed 3½ inches from each side seam, so that the distance between the straps is 6½ inches.

Repeat for the other strap on the back of the bag.

Sew the top hem of the bag in place, catching the straps as you go.

Pull the straps up, away from the bag, and topstitch around ¼ inch from the top of the bag.

DROP-CLOTH BASKET LINER

I love baskets in the kitchen for pantry organization and produce storage, and as a catchall for things that somehow make their way into this room but need to be redistributed throughout the house. My favorites are the French wicker, sea-grass, and bushel baskets that I find at antique shops. Wire egg baskets and vintage milk bottle crates also serve as the perfect vessels for storing bulk potatoes and onions.

I like to create simple basket liners because they serve as a layer of protection between ripening veggies and my favorite wicker basket, and also make it possible to store small items in baskets that have a looser weave. They are easy to clean in the washing machine, and add a pretty touch.

When my first son was a baby, I created the cheesiest matchy-matchy nursery with a handmade crib skirt, bunting, curtains, and basket liners, all in the same fabrics. Though I don't recommend following this approach, you can use basket-liner fabrics to unify mismatched baskets and bring a little coordinating accent color into a room.

I've made basket liners for circle, rectangular, and oval baskets. This is the process for making a liner for an oval vintage basket.

MATERIALS

Drop-cloth fabric (you can also use linen or cotton fabric)

If the basket is rectangular, you will have two shorter sides and two longer sides. Normally, they are angled (e.g., the bottom width measurement is 9½ inches and the top width measurement is 11¼ inches). For more-detailed photo and video instructions on a basket with these measurements, check out my How to Make a Basket Liner tutorial on farmhouseonboone.com.

INSTRUCTIONS

First, find the length and width of the bottom of the basket. If you are using a circle basket, you need the diameter.

To these measurements, add 1 inch for seam allowance. For example, the bottom of my basket measures 13 by 7 inches, so I wanted the bottom piece of drop cloth to be 14 by 8 inches.

Next, measure the length and width of the sides of the basket. For rectangular baskets with no handles, I measure the four sides and add an inch to the length and width of each for seam allowance.

The basket I've used here is more oval, so I decided to cover the inside of the basket with two pieces of drop cloth that would meet in the middle, at the handles. I measured from one side of the handle, halfway around the basket, to the handle on the other side. To this measurement I added 1 inch for seam allowance, for a total of 20 inches.

Next, I measured from the bottom of the inside of the basket to the spot where I wanted the liner to stop on

the outside. I added 1 inch for seam allowance, for a total of 10 inches.

For the tie pieces around the liner, I took the half diameter of the basket and added 16 inches. This allowed for an 8-inch overage on each side, to create the front and back ties.

For my oval basket here, these were the pieces I cut out: bottom liner piece, 14 inches by 8 inches (cut one); main liner pieces, 20 inches by 10 inches (cut two); ties around the bottom, 35 inches by 2 inches (cut two).

First, I sewed together the two main basket-liner pieces. I put the seams in the middle where the handles meet the basket. I made the seam 6 inches, instead of the full 10-inch length, because I wanted the liner to open up around the handles.

Next, I pinned the circular side piece to the bottom, all the way around.

I stitched the bottom to the side piece with a ½-inch seam. I made sure to finish the seam with a serger. (You can also use a tight zigzag stitch on a standard sewing machine.)

Next, I hemmed the open areas on the side piece that go around the handles.

Finally, I added the ties. I used a hot iron to press the raw edges of the ties inward and then in half, to hide the raw edges inside. I sandwiched the raw edge of the liner between the pressed ties. I pinned each one in place halfway around the basket, allowing for the 8-inch over-hang on each side in the front and back of the basket. I sewed the ties on the basket liner with a topstitch.

To finish the ends of the ties, I folded the short edges of each tie under and sewed around the ends with a narrow topstitch.

Finally, I fit the liner into the basket, adjusting it so that the openings lined up with the handle on each side. I used a basic double overhand knot to tie the liner on in the front and back, under the handles.

For video instructions on making a ruffle linen basket liner, visit farmhouseonboone.com.

LINEN KITCHEN APRON

Finished dimensions: Approximately 28 inches wide by 31 inches long

When beauty and utility come together in any project, my minimalist heart is pleased. My hand-made linen aprons look beautiful hanging on the wire hooks in my kitchen, and who can argue about the practicality?

As a stay-at-home mother of six who spends nearly every day buzzing around the farmhouse, an apron is a permanent fixture in my everyday wardrobe. It seems I always need to wipe my sourdough-covered hands or address a quick spill when no tea towel is in sight. The pockets are perfect for a quick trip out to the chicken coop for eggs, or when I just need to gather up the stray toys that need to make it back to the kids' rooms.

Linen is my go-to fabric of choice for basket liners, tea towels, and aprons. It has a loose weave and an excellent drape, and the fabric gets softer with each washing. Nothing says farmhouse simplicity like flax linen.

MATERIALS

2 yards of 43-inch-wide lightweight linen (or linen/cotton blend) fabric

1 spool of coordinating thread

MEASURE AND CUT

Shoulder strap pieces, 2 inches wide by 25 inches long (cut two)

Main piece, 30 inches wide by 33 inches long (cut one)

Waist strap pieces, 2 inches wide by 40 inches long (cut two)

Pocket piece, 17 inches wide by 10 inches long (cut one)

INSTRUCTIONS

On one short end of a strap piece, press over ½ inch toward the "wrong side" of the fabric. Fold the strap piece in half all the way down the long side, right sides together, and sew a ¼-inch seam.

Leave the two ends open at this point, including the short end that's folded over. Using a large safety pin at one corner, turn the strap right side out. Press the seam flat. Topstitch all along the two long sides and the folded short side, with a very narrow seam. Repeat with the other three strap pieces. *(Figure 1)*

Figure 1

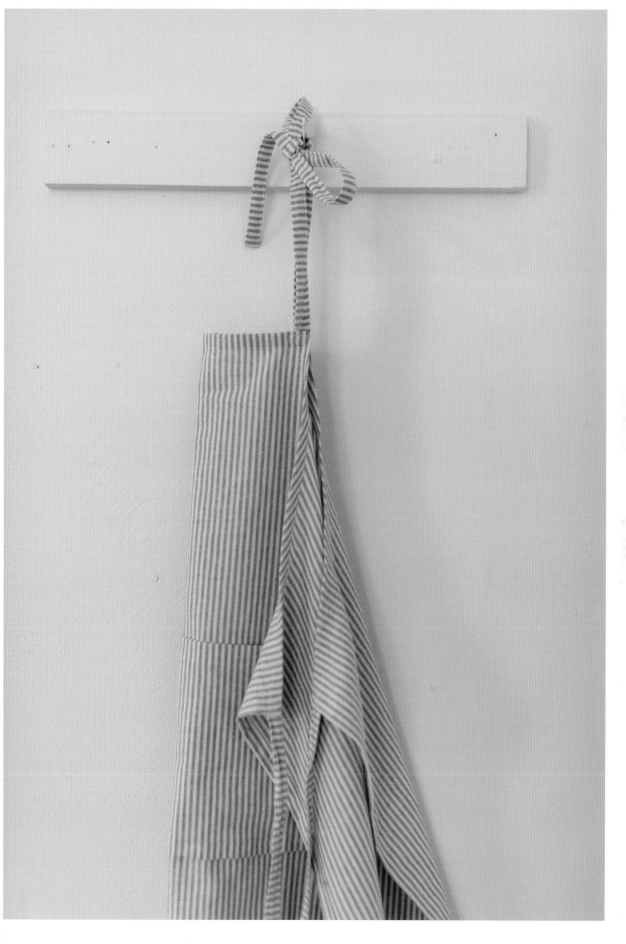

Figure 2

Figure 3

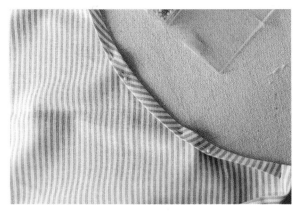

Figure 4

Fold the large rectangle in half lengthwise. At the top of the folded piece, measure 6 inches from the fold and mark with a straight pin or disappearing-ink fabric marker.

On the long side of the folded rectangle, opposite the fold, measure and mark the spot down 9 inches from the top. *(Figure 2)*

Using pins (or that fabric marker), create a curved line between the marking at the top of the rectangle and the marking on the outside. Cut along the line. This will serve as the armholes for the apron. *(Figure 3)*

Using a hot iron, press the curved armholes of the apron over ½ inch and then another ½ inch toward the wrong side of the fabric. *(Figure 4)*

Next, press the bottom and the top of the main piece over ½ inch and then another ½ inch.

Tuck the short (unfinished) end of one of the shorter strap pieces inside the pressed edge near the outside of the top of the apron, where the curved armhole meets the top. Pin in place. Repeat with the other shorter strap piece. *(Figure 5)*

Tuck the short (unfinished) end of one of the longer strap pieces inside the pressed edge near the outside of the side of the apron, where the curved armhole meets the waist. Pin in place. Repeat with the other longer strap piece.

Sew a ⅜-inch hem all the way around the main piece, catching the tucked-in straps along the way. At this point the straps are facing in toward the apron. Pull them to the outside and add a short topstitch right along the side of the apron to make the straps face away from the main piece.

Press all four sides of the pocket piece over ½ inch and then another ½ inch. Sew a hem along one long side with a ⅜-inch seam (the hemmed edge will be the top of the pocket). Center the pocket piece on the main apron piece, with the long hemmed side at the top, and pin in place.

Pocket placement: Place the short sides of the pocket piece approximately 6¼ inches from each side of the main apron piece. Place the top of the pocket 12 inches from the top of the main apron piece.

Figure 5

Sew around the three sides of the pocket piece with a ⅜-inch seam, leaving the top (hemmed edge) open. Find the center of the pocket piece and sew from the top of the pocket to the bottom, creating two pockets.

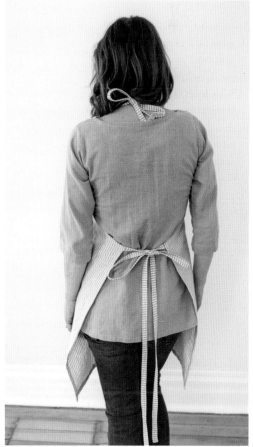

LINEN HALF APRON

Finished dimensions: Approximately 26 inches wide by 18 inches long

Sewing a half apron is a project that can be finished in half an afternoon. If you stop by the Farmhouse on Boone, you know I love a good, simple project. Don't get me wrong, I really appreciate the satisfaction that comes from crossing a mountain of a project off the list, but most the time that's just not how I roll. I need something I can whip up during nap time that will help me clean up the mess and go on to make dinner.

MATERIALS

1½ yards of 43-inch-wide lightweight linen (or linen/cotton blend) fabric

1 spool of coordinating thread

MEASURE AND CUT

Strap pieces: 50 inches wide by 5 inches long (cut two)

Main piece: 28 inches wide by 20 inches long (cut one)

Pocket piece: 20 inches wide by 12 inches tall (cut one)

INSTRUCTIONS

On one short end of a strap piece, press over ½ inch toward the "wrong side" of the fabric. Fold the strap piece in half all the way down the long side, right sides together, and sew a ¼-inch seam.

Leave the two ends open at this point, including the short end that's folded over. Using a large safety pin at one corner, turn the strap right side out. Press the seam flat. Topstitch all along the two long sides and the folded short side with a very narrow seam. Repeat with the other strap piece.

Press all four sides of the main piece over ½ inch and then another ½ inch. Sew a ⅜-inch hem on both long sides.

Tuck the short (unfinished) end of one strap piece inside the pressed edge of one short side, lining it up flush with the top (hemmed edge) of the main piece. Pin in place. Repeat with the other strap piece.

Sew a ⅜-inch hem on both short sides, catching the tucked-in straps along the way. (The straps are facing in toward the apron.) Pull them to the outside and add a short topstitch right along the side of the apron to make the straps face away from the main piece.

Press all four sides of the pocket piece over ½ inch and then another inch. Sew a ⅜-inch hem along one long side with a ⅜-inch seam. (The hemmed edge will be the top of the pocket.) Center the pocket piece on the main apron piece, with the long hemmed side at the top, and pin in place.

Pocket placement: Place the short sides of the pocket piece 4 inches from each side of the main apron piece. Place the top of the pocket 4 inches from the top of the main apron piece.

Sew around the three sides of the pocket piece with a ⅜-inch seam, leaving the top (hemmed edge) open. Find the center of the pocket piece and sew from the top of the pocket to the bottom, creating two pockets.

LINEN PINAFORE APRON

I have a few pinafore aprons in my collection. They are simple and old-fashioned, and offer your clothing full protection from bone-broth splashes and messy toddler hands.

MATERIALS

2 yards linen, cotton, or linen/cotton blend fabric

MEASURE, MARK, AND CUT

Straps, 21 inches long by 7½ inches wide (cut two)

Main piece, 35 inches long by 41 inches wide (cut one)

Pockets, 10 inches by 10 inches (cut two)

INSTRUCTIONS

Take one strap piece and fold it in half, with right sides together. Sew the raw edges together all the way down the long edge with a ½-inch seam. Turn the strap piece out so that the raw edges, and seam, are hidden inside. Do this by placing a large safety pin on one end and fishing it through to the other end. Press the strap with an iron to make the seams lay flat. Topstitch on both long edges of the strap (the folded edge and the seam side). Repeat with the other strap piece.

Press all four edges of a 10-by-10-inch pocket piece over ½ inch, and then another ½ inch, to hide the raw edges inside. Sew one edge of the pocket piece, to create a hem. This will be the top of the pocket. Leave the other three edges unsewn, as these will be sewn directly onto the main piece of the apron. Repeat with the other pocket piece.

For the main apron piece, press all four sides over ½ inch, and then another ½ inch, to hide the raw edges inside. Sew down the two short sides and one long side with a ⅜-inch hem. Leave the top unsewn.

Take one strap and pin it 13½ inches from the side hemmed edge of the main apron piece. Put it underneath the pressed top edge of the main piece. This is the one that you left unsewn earlier. Take the other strap piece and pin it 13½ inches from the other edge of the main piece. The two strap pieces should be about 6 inches apart.

You will notice that the straps face down toward the main apron piece. To make them face up, away from the apron, flip them up and then sew close to the top of the apron to make them stay put.

Turn the apron over. Take the strap on the left and crisscross it over to meet the outside edge of the main apron piece on the opposite side. Pin the strap in place. Repeat with the strap on the right, crisscrossing it over to the other outside edge. Sew the straps that are lined up with the outside edge in place. Flip them up, away from the main apron piece, and sew along the top to keep them up.

Place the hemmed top of the pocket 14 inches from the hemmed top of the main apron piece. Line up the side of the pocket 10 inches from the hemmed outside edge of the main apron piece. Repeat with the other pocket. The two pockets should be 2¾ inches apart.

Sew around the three sides of the pocket, leaving the hemmed edge (the top of the pocket) open.

PINAFORE APRON FOR KIDS

This is just like the adult version, but with a ruffle on the bottom! It's perfect for those little helpers who love getting messy in the kitchen.

MATERIALS

1 yard linen, cotton, or linen/cotton blend fabric

MEASURE, MARK, AND CUT

Sizes 2–4: Main piece, 18 inches long by 30 inches wide (cut one); straps, 11 inches long by 4½ inches wide (cut two); ruffle, 45 inches by 5½ inches inches (cut one); pockets, 5½ inches by 5½ inches (cut two)

Sizes 4–6: Main piece, 20 inches long by 32 inches wide (cut one); straps, 13 inches long by 5 inches wide (cut two); ruffle, 48 inches by 6 inches (cut one); pockets, 6 inches by 6 inches (cut two)

Sizes 6–8: Main piece, 22 inches long by 34 inches wide (cut one); straps, 15 inches long by 5½ inches wide (cut two); ruffle, 51 inches by 6½ inches (cut one); pockets 6½ inches by 6½ inches (cut two)

Sizes 8–10: Main piece, 24 inches long by 36 inches wide (cut one); straps, 17 inches long by 6 inches wide (cut two); ruffle, 54 inches by 7 inches (cut one); pockets 7 inches by 7 inches (cut two)

INSTRUCTIONS

Take one strap piece and fold it in half, with right sides together. Sew the raw edges together all the way down the long edge with a ¼-inch seam. Turn the strap piece out, so that the raw edges, and seam, are hidden inside. Do this by placing a large safety pin on one end and fishing it through to the other end. Press the strap flat with an iron to make the seams lay flat. Topstitch on both long edges of the strap (the folded edge and the side with the seam). Repeat with the other strap piece.

Press all four edges of a pocket piece over ½ inch, and then another ½ inch, to hide the raw edges inside. Sew one edge of the pocket piece, to create a hem. This will be the top of the pocket. Leave the other three edges unsewn, as these will be sewn directly onto the main piece of the apron. Repeat with the other pocket piece.

Prepare the main piece of the apron. Press, along the sides and top, to the back, ½ inch, and then another ½ inch, to hide the raw edges inside. Don't press the bottom. We will leave that raw to attach the ruffle to later. Sew down the sides with a ⅜-inch hem. Leave the top unsewn at this time.

Place the strap pieces underneath the pressed area at the top, lined up with the outside edges of the apron. Sew the straps in place. Cross the straps over each other, so they are crisscrossed. Pin the straps in place toward the middle of the front of the apron. (Refer to the Pocket- and Strap-Placement Guide on the next page to find out how far to pin the straps in from the outside edge of the main piece.) Sew the front straps in place under the top pressed edge. Flip them up, away from the main apron piece, and sew along the top to keep them up.

To pin the pockets in place, refer to the Pocket- and Strap-Placement Guide on the next page. Remember that the part you already stitched will be the top of the pocket. Sew the pocket in place around the three sides, leaving the top open.

Hem one long edge and both short edges of the ruffle piece with a ½-inch hem. Add a gathering stitch to the other long edge, and gather the ruffle until its length matches the width of the bottom of the apron. Pin the ruffle, with right sides together, to the bottom of the apron, and sew it in place. Finish the raw edges, where the ruffle joins with the apron, with a zigzag stitch or serger. Topstitch the ruffle to make it lay flat.

POCKET-AND
STRAP-PLACEMENT GUIDE

Since there will always be a slight variation in the size of the seams and pattern cutting, use the following measurements as guides only. The pockets and straps should be centered on the apron.

Sizes 2–4: The top of the pocket should be placed 6 inches from the top of the apron. Place the outside edge of the pocket 6½ inches from the outside edge of the apron. Put the back straps in flush with the outside of the main apron piece. Place the outside edges of the front straps in 10 inches from the outside of the apron. They should be 3½ inches apart in the front.

Sizes 4–6: The top of the pocket should be placed 8 inches from the top of the apron. Place the outside edge of the pocket 8½ inches from the outside edge of the apron. Put the back straps in flush with the outside of the main apron piece. Place the outside edges of the front straps in 10½ inches from the outside of the apron. They should be 4½ inches apart in the front.

Sizes 6–8: The top of the pocket should be placed 10 inches from the top of the apron. Place the outside edge of the pocket 9½ inches from the outside edge of the apron. Put the back straps in flush with the outside of the main apron piece. Place the outside edges of the front straps in 10¾ inches from the outside of the apron. They should be 5½ inches apart in the front.

Sizes 8–10: The top of the pocket should be placed 12 inches from the top of the apron. Place the outside edge of the pocket 10½ inches from the outside edge of the apron. Put the back straps in flush with the outside of the main apron piece. Place the outside edges of the front straps in 11 inches from the outside of the apron. They should be 6½ inches apart in the front.

FRUIT AND VEGGIE WASH

We love growing vegetables in our backyard garden, but we still rely on the good old grocery store for a lot of our produce. Although I'm very thankful we have the option, I am not always sure how the store-bought produce is grown, especially the nonorganic fruits and veggies. One way to decrease pesticide residue is to thoroughly scrub produce with fresh water and a simple produce wash. If I could choose only one essential oil for my home, it would be lemon. The antimicrobial citrus works beautifully to cleanse in a natural way.

INGREDIENTS

2 cups filtered water

½ cup distilled white vinegar

5 drops lemon essential oil

INSTRUCTIONS

Combine all of the ingredients in a glass spray bottle and give it a good shake. For best results, spray the solution on the produce and allow it to sit on the surface for 5 to 10 minutes before scrubbing it with a tea towel.

Tip: For greens, herbs, and softer fruits and veggies, you can use a similar formulation as a soak. Combine the ingredients in a large bowl and submerge your produce in the water, vinegar, and lemon mixture. Allow it to soak for 5 to 10 minutes. Strain and rinse the produce in a colander.

LEMON ROSEMARY FOAMING HAND AND DISH SOAP

This little soap recipe is a workhorse here in our home. I use it for everything from cleaning hands and high chairs to removing countertop stains and washing dishes. The lemon essential oil is excellent at cutting grime and removing stains. I use a touch of rosemary for its garden-fresh scent and natural antibacterial properties. When our white farmhouse sink is looking dirty, I just squirt this soap all over and allow it to soak for about 15 minutes. The grime miraculously wipes away. It has completely replaced our need for dish soap as well. The foaming dispenser makes a little go a long way when I'm hand-washing dishes for my family of seven.

INGREDIENTS

Unscented castile soap
Filtered water
10 drops lemon essential oil
3 drops rosemary essential oil

OTHER SUPPLIES

Foaming hand soap dispenser

INSTRUCTIONS

Fill the foaming hand soap container one-quarter of the way with castile soap.

Add the essential oils.

Fill the rest of the way with water.

CAST-IRON SALT SCRUB

There are only two things that get better with age in the kitchen: one is a homemade sourdough starter, and the other, a well-seasoned cast-iron skillet. If you stopped by our farmhouse, you would certainly see a stack at least three deep sitting on top of the stove. For a perfectly fried egg, potatoes so crispy you can hear the crunch, or a caramelized sear on a roast to seal in all of those delicious juices, you just can't beat the performance of cast iron.

There are a few rules to cleaning cast iron, leading many people to believe it's high-maintenance. Nothing can be further from the truth. Once your skillet is well seasoned and you master a very basic cleaning routine, you will find cast iron is actually easier to maintain than stainless-steel and nonstick pans.

If nothing is sticking to the pan, you can simply wipe it out until the next use. If something gets really stuck on, you can use this slightly abrasive cast-iron salt scrub to get a little scrubbing power behind all of that elbow grease. Scoop a couple teaspoons of the salt mixture onto the pan. Use a microfiber cloth, or scrub sponge, to work it in. Once all the food is loose, rinse the skillet in warm water. Use a tea towel to wipe off any excess water. The pan should be completely dry before putting it away.

The two rules of cleaning cast iron are:
1. Don't use soap.
2. Make sure every part of the pan is dried thoroughly.

INGREDIENTS

1 cup coarse salt

**2 tablespoons almond or
    fractionated* coconut oil**

20 drops lemon essential oil

*** A type of coconut oil that stays
    liquid at room temperature.**

INSTRUCTIONS

Combine all the ingredients in a small Mason jar. Store the scrub next to your stove for extra cleaning power next time you have a cast-iron mess on your hands.

WOODEN SPOON BUTTER

Next to cast-iron skillets, a small collection of stainless-steel pots, and a hefty stockpile of glass storage containers, wooden cutting boards and utensils are some of the most-used essentials in my natural kitchen. Wooden spoons are great for everything from feeding my sourdough starter to dishing up a bowl of homemade rustic granola, and wooden cutting boards are all I use for chopping veggies. They are charming in a farmhouse kitchen lined up on the counter, the utensils displayed in chipped vintage crocks. You can find the most beautiful cutting boards and hand-carved rustic spoons from makers and small family shops online. Just like with cast iron, they last forever if you know how to properly care for them.

INGREDIENTS

3 tablespoons organic beeswax pellets, or wax from a local beekeeper cut into large pieces

10 tablespoons coconut oil (You can also use flaxseed, olive, sunflower, almond, or walnut oil. I opt for coconut oil, because I always have it around, and it's not likely to go rancid as quickly as something like olive oil.)

INSTRUCTIONS

Add the beeswax and coconut oil to a wide-mouth Mason jar.

Place a folded tea towel or trivet in the bottom of a medium pot. Add a couple inches of water and heat it over medium heat until it comes to a simmer. Place the Mason jar into it.

Heat the ingredients until they are fully melted.

Remove the jar from the heat and give it a vigorous stir with the handle end of a wooden spoon. If you have a skinny wooden spoon that will fit inside the Mason jar, you can use that also.

Once the mixture cools, you are free to begin using it on all of your wooden spoons, cutting boards, rolling pins, and bowls.

HOW TO CARE FOR WOODEN UTENSILS IN THE KITCHEN

Hand-wash them with a mild soap, like my Lemon Rosemary Foaming Hand and Dish Soap on page 30, and warm water.

Dry them thoroughly with a tea towel, so the water doesn't have a chance to damage them or cause any mold to form.

Use the Wooden Spoon Butter recipe on an as-needed basis whenever your cutting boards, spoons, or rolling pins start to look a little dry. Use your hands to rub a layer over the entire piece and allow it to soak in for several hours.

Next time you go to use a previously oiled utensil, wipe any excess spoon butter away with a tea towel.

Instead of composting citrus peels and excess garden herbs, use them in a simmering stovetop potpourri!

SIMMERING STOVETOP POTPOURRI

When I was pregnant with my first daughter, there was a certain plug-in air freshener that made me feel nauseated every time I got near it. After some research, I now know that my body was trying to tell me something. Those things are toxic. They are full of phthalates, which disrupt hormones and can cause reproductive problems. Yikes! Good thing there are so many natural ways to hide the fact that you made fish for dinner last night and changed no less than five stinky diapers today. We often have a diffuser with our favorite essential oil blends going in the kitchen, but simmering stovetop potpourri is another favorite way to make the place smell like we spent all day cleaning.

INGREDIENTS

Any combination of fruit, spices, herbs, and essential oils works great, but here are a few combinations to get you started:

Lemon, rosemary, and vanilla beans (or extract)

Lavender, lemon, and sage

Mint, lime, and thyme

Apple, lemon, and vanilla beans (or extract)

Clove, orange, and cinnamon sticks

INSTRUCTIONS

Add a handful of herbs and a couple of sliced fruits to a medium stockpot.

Add 4 cups of water and bring it to a boil. Reduce the heat to low and simmer for several hours.

Add more water as needed throughout the day.

> Tip: Add a few drops of essential oil to make the scent even stronger.

CHAPTER 2

HANDMADE HOME

WHEN WE BOUGHT OUR FIRST HOME, my design approach could best be described as "Craigslist free section chic." If someone gave it to us, I was determined to make it work. I quickly learned that good old paint covered a multitude of design sins, and on the cheap. It took us ten years to completely transform that place, but we had it looking significantly better in just a few weeks, thanks to many 5-gallon buckets of paint.

Sea-grass and wicker baskets add to my minimal aesthetic, and are perfect for storing unsightly things, like remote controls and puzzles. Nowadays, I like to keep a few nice pieces in each room, like our big farm table and benches, rather than clutter things up with a half-pretty garage-sale bargain.

My favorite way to add a handmade touch to our home is by sewing pillow covers, blankets, dresses, aprons, and tote bags. With just a few basic skills—like learning how to stitch a seam, sew a hem, and use a gathering stitch to make a pretty ruffle—it is very simple to create something for every room in your home.

I love that when I look around our farmhouse, it's hard to find an area where there *isn't* something I spent time working on with my hands as a way to put my own personal stamp on it. This makes a home feel collected, cozy, and unique.

DIPPED BEESWAX CANDLES

There is something in my "back to our roots" personality that wants to know how everything is made on the most basic level.

I started making hand-poured and -dipped candles to satisfy my curiosity for this ancient practice. Handmade taper candles have such a simple and rustic beauty, and I love the process of taking the raw material of beeswax to create something useful. The earthy yellow color of these candles looks charming on a windowsill or lined up on a big farmhouse table.

Store-bought candles are usually made from paraffin wax, which is a waste product of petroleum. While these "regular" candles create indoor air pollution, beeswax candles release negative ions and actually purify the air.

MATERIALS

3 pounds beeswax pellets, or wax from a local beekeeper cut into large pieces

One length of 90- to 100-inch braided candlewick

Deep and narrow container, such as a wide-mouth Mason jar

Stockpot

Hex nut (for a weight)

As you are making candles, the wax level will continue to decrease with each candle dipped. At some point, you may want to pour wax from one jar to the other two, so that you can maintain the depth for uniform-looking candles.

When the wax level is at a point where it will no longer make a pretty candle, pour it into a silicone baking mold to harden and save for future projects.

INSTRUCTIONS

Put the beeswax pellets into a wide-mouth Mason jar or a tall metal tin. Make sure whatever container you are using is narrow, so the wax is deep. I like to use three 24-ounce wide-mouth Mason jars, because they are the perfect height to create 6- to 7-inch taper candles.

Place a folded tea towel or trivet in the bottom of a medium to large stockpot. Add 3 to 4 inches of water and heat it over medium heat, until it comes to a simmer. Place the jar (or jars) of wax into it. You will be able to add more wax as the pellets melt down.

Cut four wicks 25 inches in length. On each one tie a hex nut on both ends.

Once the wax in the jars is melted, it is time to start dipping. To do this, hold each wick in the center and slowly dip the ends into the wax. After each dip into the hot wax, dip the wicks into a jar of cold water. This will speed up the cooling process.

Go back and forth about ten times until the candle has enough weight to be fully submerged without the hex nut. Cut off the weights at the bottom and continue going back and forth between the wax and the water until the candle has reached the desired diameter.

Allow the candles to harden by placing them on wax paper, in a cool dry spot, for a few hours.

Before burning the candles, trim the wick to about ¼ inch in length.

BASIC PILLOW COVER TUTORIAL

Finished dimensions: 20 inches by 20 inches

Basic pillow covers are the perfect project for beginners. With just three rectangular pieces, straight lines, and no fancy gathering stitches or sewing jargon, you can learn how to make them, no matter what your current skill level is.

After a while, vintage grain sacks and sheets, stonewashed linen, and repurposed knit sweaters will all look like great pillow material to you. Your mind will wander toward all of the possibilities for every room in your home. Don't say I didn't warn you! Once you know your way around your sewing machine, you may start adding ties, ruffles, pleats, and piping.

For now, let's learn how to sew a basic pillow cover.

MATERIALS

1 yard cotton fabric

MEASURE AND CUT

Back pieces, 13 inches wide by 21 inches tall (cut two)

Main piece, 21 inches wide by 21 inches tall (cut one)

INSTRUCTIONS

Prepare the two back pieces. Take one of the 21-by-13-inch pieces and fold it over ½ inch on the 21-inch side. Iron it in place. Fold over the 21-inch side another ½ inch and iron in place, hiding the raw edge inside. Repeat for the other 21-by-13-inch piece. Stitch the hems all the way down with a ⅜-inch hem.

Sew the two back pieces to the front piece. Put the 21-inch square piece down with the right side of the fabric facing up. Lay the two back pieces on the main

TIPS FOR GETTING THE RIGHT PILLOW INSERTS

My favorite inserts are made from down, or a down alternative. They are extra full and cozy, but they can sometimes be a little pricier.

In my early sewing days, I grabbed mismatched zebra print, 1980s floral patterns, and hot pink faux fur pillows from the thrift shop. Charcoal gray–dyed drop cloth hid the colors underneath, and cozy pillows graced our home for less than a couple of dollars each.

You can also buy new polyester pillow inserts for around five bucks apiece, but they are usually a little thin and lifeless. For a fuller look, make sure to size up when adding the pillow insert. For a 20-by-20-inch pillow cover, I recommend purchasing a 22-inch polyester pillow form.

front piece, with right sides together. Overlap the two back pieces, so that all the raw edges are lined up. The two hemmed sides of the back pieces should be in the middle. Pin everything in place. Stitch all the way around the pillow cover with a ½-inch seam.

Go around the pillow cover with a zigzag stitch to finish off the raw edges.

Turn the pillow cover right side out, making sure to push out the corners.

CUSTOM INSERT

When making pillow covers from vintage materials, it is hard to find an insert that is just the perfect size for that beautiful 1920s grain sack you scored. Creating a custom insert is simple and inexpensive, and requires just a few basic materials.

MATERIALS

1 yard canvas, linen, or cotton fabric
Polyester fiberfill, down alternative, or feather down

INSTRUCTIONS

Measure the size of your finished pillow cover.

Add 1 inch to the width and 1 inch to the length. This will allow for a ½-inch seam allowance on all four sides when you go to sew your front and back pieces together.

If you want the pillow insert to be slightly longer so that it peeks out the other side, you can add an extra ½ inch to 1 inch to the length measurement.

Cut out two pieces of fabric in the dimensions you came up with. (Length and width of the pillow cover plus 1 inch on the length and width.)

Sew the two pieces together with a ½-inch seam all the way around, leaving a 3-inch opening.

Turn it right side out, making sure to poke out all the corners with your fingers.

Add stuffing until it is full enough for your liking. I prefer a down alternative, as it looks cozy and full.

Add a topstitch to close up the 3-inch opening.

GRAIN-SACK AND TICKING-STRIPE PILLOW COVER

Once you master the Basic Pillow Cover tutorial (see page 43), try layering on a simple grain-sack tie pillow cover.

MATERIALS

Two 18-inch pieces of ½-inch double-fold bias tape

Two 21-by-21-inch pieces of grain-sack fabric (Make sure the stripes on the fabric are centered when you are cutting them out. For this particular fabric, the stripes are 10 inches apart, so I have 3¼ inches between the edge of the stripe and the end of the fabric.)

INSTRUCTIONS

Prepare the bias-tape ties. Take one of the 18-inch pieces of double-fold bias tape and fold one end under. Sew that folded end in place, and then all the way down the open (non-folded) side of the bias tape. Repeat for the other 18-inch piece of bias tape.

Place the two grain-sack squares on top of each other, with right sides together. If the grain sack you are using has stripes, it is important to line them up ahead of time. Sew three-quarters of the way around with a ⅜-inch seam, leaving one side open. This will be the side that will have the ties. Finish the seams with a serger or zigzag stitch.

On the side that you left open, find the exact middle and use a disappearing-ink fabric marker or straight pin to mark that spot on both the front and the back pieces. This is where the ties will go, since you want them centered in the middle of the pillow.

Fold the side that was left open over to the inside of the pillow cover ¼ inch, and then fold in again another ¼ inch, to hide the raw edge inside.

Begin sewing around until you reach the place that you marked as the center. This is where you will sew in the first tie. (**Note:** Normally I would press the edge over with my iron to create a seam like this, but the grain-sack fabric is so thick that I find it does not press well. Instead, I just fold it down as I go around. You could also use straight pins.)

Tuck the unfinished end of one of the 18-inch bias-tape ties into the hem that you are making around the opening of the grain-sack pillow cover. Continue sewing around until you reach the other marking and repeat the process to sew in the other tie.

After you have sewn all the way around, go back over the spots where the ties are and sew them over to the outside of the pillow.

First, add a ticking-stripe pillow cover made from the Basic Pillow Cover tutorial on page 43. Layer on top of that the grain-sack tie pillow cover. Make a little bow with the ties, and enjoy!

HOW TO SEW A RUFFLE

When you are comfortable with making a basic pillow cover, throw blanket, or apron, you may want to start adding a little more frill with some ruffles. I have never really been a girly girl, but when it comes to ruffles, I just can't help myself. I add them to slipcovers, curtains, and tea towels, and sometimes I add multiple layers of them onto the bottoms of dresses for my girls. Projects usually don't look complete without a ruffle or pleat finishing off the hemline. I know a lot of beginners think that ruffles are intimidating and difficult, but once you get the hang of it, you too will be adding them to everything.

MATERIALS

You will need a strip of fabric that has a similar weight to the project you will be attaching it to.

INSTRUCTIONS

To determine the width of the ruffle piece, take the length you want to add to the project and add 1½ inches to it. For example, if you'd like to have a total length (from shoulder to hemline) of 36 inches for your dress, and the dress has a length (before the ruffle) of 30 inches, you will want the ruffle piece to be 7½ inches long. This will allow for ½ inch where the ruffle will be attached to the project, and another inch for the hemline.

The rule of thumb for length of the ruffle piece is one and a half times the piece that you are attaching it to. So, using the same example above, let's say your dress was made up of two skirt pieces, each 20 inches wide. You will cut two strips that are each 30 inches wide for the ruffle pieces.

Before gathering, create the hem in the bottom of the ruffle piece. I like to do this first while the strip is straight and flat, not all ruffled up. Press the long edge over ½ inch and then another ½ inch, and then sew a ⅜-inch hem all the way down.

To make sure that the sides (short edges) of the ruffle piece are not left raw, they need to be finished. The way this is accomplished will depend on what you are sewing the ruffle to. If it is going on a dress, like in the example on the next page, you will simply sew two ruffle pieces at the side seams with right sides together.

If there is only one ruffle piece and it will not be attached at the sides to anything else, like on the

Light- to medium-weight fabrics, like cotton, linen, and washed drop cloth, make prettier ruffles than heavyweight fabrics.

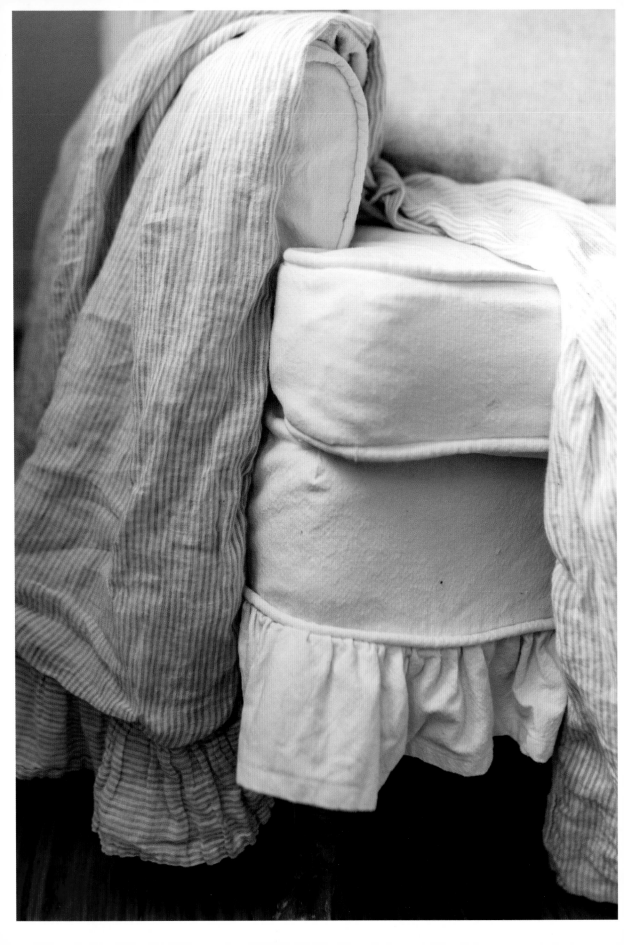

bottom of an apron, just create a small hem on both sides of the ruffle piece.

If you are attaching the ruffle in a circular fashion—around a pillow cover, for example—you will attach the two short edges of one long ruffle piece with right sides together.

Set your machine tension, and the stitch length, to the highest setting.

Sew a straight line along the top of the strip (the non-hemmed edge), ⅜ inch from the edge, leaving long tails of thread at each end. Make sure not to backstitch. Gently pull on one of the threads on the tail end of the gathering stitch to begin creating little gathers in the fabric.

Continue sliding the fabric along the stitch, being careful not to tug too hard and break the thread. Continue gathering until the length of the ruffle matches the length of the item you are sewing it to.

Use straight pins to attach the ruffle to the piece of fabric you are sewing it to, with right sides together. Turn the machine tension and stitch length back down to the manufacturer settings, and sew the ruffle on with about a ½-inch seam.

If you are creating a superlong ruffle strip—say, for the bottom of a chair slipcover—it is wise to create several gathering stitches along the way. Be sure to keep the gathering stitches no longer than 50 inches; this will help to keep them from breaking.

Sew just over the gathering stitch, so that it is hidden inside, but as close as possible to it. The further you get away from the original gathering stitch, the more likely you are to get awkward puckers and weird spacing in the gathers.

CROCHET-TRIM DOUBLE-GAUZE THROW BLANKET

Finished dimensions: 70 inches by 50 inches

Throw blankets are a simple way to brighten up a home and add cozy textures. We have one draped over every chair arm and bedframe in the farmhouse. When sewing soft goods for our home, I almost always reach for cotton, linen, flannel, or gauze. Double gauze is a double-woven cotton fabric with an open weave. Like a lightweight linen, it has a beautiful soft drape. It gets a little softer with each wash and wears beautifully over time. This cotton gauze blanket features a soft crochet detail to give it an antique heirloom feel. My favorite part of this project is no fabric or trim goes to waste. It is a simple and quick project that will be enjoyed for years to come.

MATERIALS

4 yards 52-inch-wide double-gauze fabric

3 yards crochet cotton lace trim

INSTRUCTIONS

Fold the fabric in half the long way and cut down the middle, so that you're left with two pieces, each 52 inches by 72 inches.

Cut the crochet cotton lace trim in half, so that you have two 54-inch pieces.

Working on the short edge of the gauze fabric, pin the edge of the trim ⅜ inch from the edge of the fabric, and sew in place. (*Figure 1*)

Figure 1

Repeat with the other piece of trim on the other end of the same gauze piece.

Place the other piece of double gauze on top of the trim piece, right sides together, with the cotton crochet trim sandwiched in between. *(Figure 2)*

Sew all the way around with a ½-inch seam. Leave a 4-inch spot open, on one side of the throw blanket, to pull it right side out. Round the corners, and make sure that the ends of the trim pieces are sticking out beyond the seams.

Pull the blanket right side out.

Finish with a topstitch all the way around, being sure to close up the 4-inch spot that was left open.

Figure 2

LINEN RUFFLE THROW BLANKET

Finished dimensions: 79 inches by 45 inches

I have made this blanket more than once, and plan to try it a few more times with different shades of linen. It drapes beautifully over the edge of a bed or chair, and looks lovely spilling out of a wicker basket. I can imagine it in a dramatic charcoal black, or a soft blush linen solid on cream flannel.

Thinking about a throw made in a checked-grid pattern, wide yarn-dyed stripe, or one of the many pale, faded neutrals, makes me want to spend a day locked in the craft room to bring the many possibilities to life. What if the main linen on the blanket was a natural oatmeal color and the ruffle a dusty rose? Oh, and it could have double ruffles on the ends, or pleats! I'm getting carried away.

MATERIALS

2 yards 58-inch-wide lightweight linen, or linen/cotton blend

1½ yards 108-inch-wide flannel

MEASURE, MARK, AND CUT

One 70-by-46-inch piece of linen

One 70-by-46-inch piece of flannel

Two 70-by-6-inch pieces for the ruffles

INSTRUCTIONS

Linen and flannel shrink in different ways, so even if you cut the front and back pieces exactly the same size, they may end up as different sizes after the first trip through the dryer. You can plan to always wash your blanket on cold and hang it out to dry to avoid shrinkage, but we have a few too many hands in the laundry room to ensure proper care, so prewashing and drying is a better option in my house! The first time I made this blanket, I skipped this step, meaning the linen wraps a bit around the front, as the flannel back is now smaller. Nonetheless, it's still one of my favorite blankets in the house.

The linen fabric is 58 inches wide, so you will have a 12-by-70-inch strip left after cutting your 46-by-70-inch piece. Cut that long leftover piece in half down the middle and you will have your two ruffle pieces.

Press the long side of one ruffle piece ¼ inch and then another ¼ inch, toward the wrong side of the fabric, to hide the raw edges inside. Sew the hem down the entire length of the long side of the ruffle piece. Next, press both short ends over ¼ inch and then another ¼ inch, to hide the raw edges inside. Sew the hems down on both short ends so that you have three edges hemmed. Next, put a gathering stitch in the long side of the ruffle piece that wasn't hemmed. Tug the strings gently from both ends to create a 46-inch ruffle, the length of the short end of the large linen piece. Repeat the above steps for the other ruffle piece.

Pin one ruffle to one short end of the linen piece, with right sides together. Instead of lining up the raw edges, the ruffle should be at least ¼ inch away from the edge of the main linen piece. You will need that extra space to sew the flannel to the linen later. Sew the ruffle in place, being careful to sew closely to the gathering stitch. Repeat with the other ruffle piece on the other short edge of the main linen piece.

To keep the ruffles away from the edges while sewing, fold them over and secure them with straight pins. Lay the linen piece on the floor with the right side facing up and the ruffles facing down, and lay the flannel piece on top. Secure the front to the back with straight pins. Sew around the entire thing with a ⅜-inch seam, leaving one 4-inch area open. Be sure to not sew too far away from the original ruffle stitch on the short ends. Turn the blanket right side out, through the 4-inch opening. To close up the opening, fold the flannel and linen under and put in a topstitch.

I'm a sucker for a topstitch. Seeing those straight lines in coordinating thread just makes something look more finished to me. Your blanket will hold up just fine without this step, if you decide to skip it!

REVERSIBLE DROP-CLOTH THROW

Finished dimensions: 73 inches by 47 inches

Drop cloth is one of the most versatile and inexpensive fabrics for the home sewist. I use it in every-thing from curtains and slipcovers to pillows and table runners. It is a nice medium weight that is perfect for home decor. It can be bleached, dyed, painted, or just used with its natural linen color. After drop cloth has been washed and dried several times, it is transformed from a coarse texture to something surprisingly soft.

I lined this casual throw with flannel, so that the back is snuggly and soft and the front is the neutral that I love so much in our farmhouse decor. A little flannel peeks out around the edges, adding contrast and a touch of color. You could also choose to display this blanket on the flannel side when you want to bring in a little more pattern. I used bleached drop cloth for my blanket. You can also dye it (see page 70). Imagine—so many possibilities!

MATERIALS

3 yards 46-inch-wide flannel fabric

One 72-by-46-inch piece of drop cloth (prewashed and dried)

MEASURE AND CUT

Main drop-cloth piece, 72 inches long by 46 inches wide

Main flannel piece, 72 inches long by 46 inches wide

Ruffle piece, 350 inches long by 4 inches wide

(Note: Since you will not have a piece that is 350 inches long, you can join several strips together, with a ¼-inch seam, to reach the ruffle length. Press the seams open flat.)

INSTRUCTIONS

Cut out a large 72-by-46-inch piece of flannel. Lay the flannel on top of the drop cloth and round off all four corners slightly, with your scissors. Press ½ inch toward the wrong side of the drop-cloth fabric, working all the way around the entire piece. Repeat with the flannel fabric.

Sew the ends of the 350-inch ruffle piece together, so that you have a long circle. Fold the ruffle piece in half, with wrong sides together, and press flat. Put a gathering stitch in the top (non-folded edge) of the ruffle piece. (For a piece this long, I prefer to put in about seven separate gathering stitches, approximately every 50 inches. This ensures that I won't break the strings on one long gathering stitch.)

OPTION 1 (MORE ADVANCED)

With wrong sides together, lay the flannel piece on top of the drop-cloth piece, lining up the pressed edges all the way around. Gather the ruffle with the loose gathering stitch, until the diameter of the ruffle matches the diameter around the blanket. Sandwich the gathered end of the ruffle piece between the drop-cloth and flannel pieces and pin in place. Topstitch all the way around, catching the main drop-cloth piece, the main flannel piece, and the ruffle. Make sure to back- and forward-stitch at the beginning and end.

OPTION 2 (FOR BEGINNERS)

This method requires going all the way around the blanket twice, sewing it in sections. This ensures that you will catch all the layers. Gather the ruffle with the loose gathering stitch, until the diameter of the ruffle matches the diameter around the blanket. Lay the ruffle on top of the drop-cloth piece, with the gathered edge of the ruffle on the pressed edge of the drop-cloth piece and the folded edge of the ruffle facing outward. Pin in place. Sew all the way around, attaching the ruffle to the drop-cloth piece. Lay the flannel piece on top of the drop-cloth piece, sandwiching the ruffle in between. Sew all the way around, being sure to line up the sides and rounded corners. Make sure to back- and forward-stitch at the beginning and end.

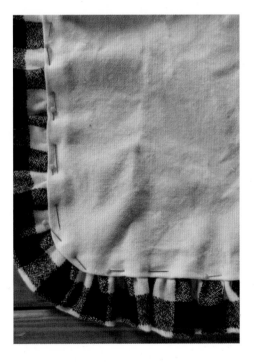

TIE-TOP LINEN CURTAINS

Draped in a little puddle on the floor, linen curtains are just the kind of soft and neutral window treatment that an antique farmhouse needs. Linen is flowy enough to look unstuffy, but not so totally sheer that a closed curtain can't block a little light. Even after you iron it, the woven-flax textile in all of its casual and imperfect glory still looks a little crinkly. The ties at the top of these curtains make them soft, airy, and a little romantic.

MATERIALS

7 yards 58-inch-wide medium-weight linen or linen/cotton blend

INSTRUCTIONS

Measure your window and cut out the pieces. We have very tall ceilings in our old farmhouse, so my curtains may be a little longer than yours. I wanted to hang mine about 3 inches above the window and have a bit of a puddle on the floor, so I needed the total finished curtain length to be 104 inches. I put in a ½-inch hem on the top of the curtain panels and a 1½-inch hem on the bottom. The ties add 4 inches to the total length.

So here is how I got the main curtain-panel length:

$$104 + 3 \text{ (1½-inch hem} \times 2) + 1 \text{ (½-inch hem} \times 2) - 4 \text{ (tie length)} = 104$$

I just used the width of the linen, so I ended up with two large pieces, 104 inches by 58 inches, for my main curtain-panel pieces.

For the ties, cut twenty strips of linen 18 inches by 1½ inches. On one short end of a tie piece, press over ½ inch toward the wrong side of the fabric. Fold the tie piece in half all the way down the long side, right sides together, and sew a ¼-inch seam. Leave the two ends open at this point, including the short end that's folded over. Using a large safety pin at one corner, turn the strap right side out. Press the seam flat. Topstitch all along the two long sides and the folded short side, with a very narrow seam. Repeat for the other nineteen tie pieces.

Press the top, and two sides, of one of the main pieces over ½ inch and then another ½ inch. Press the bottom over 1½ inches and then another 1½ inches toward the wrong side. Sew a ⅜-inch hem down both long sides. Sew a 1⅜-inch hem at the bottom. Leave the top open at this point.

Tuck the unfinished edges of two tie pieces under the top ½-inch pressed edge, flush with the outside of the main curtain piece. Do the same on the other side of the top edge. At this point you should have four tie pieces tucked in, two on one top edge and two on the other. Pin the ties in place.

Fold the curtain in half and mark the middle. Place another two ties in the middle, and pin in place. Fold the middle to one of the outside edges, and mark the center. Tuck in two more ties and pin in place. Do the same with the middle and the other outside edge. You will now have five sets of two ties evenly spaced out along the top of one curtain panel, and tucked in under the pressed edge. Sew along the top with a ⅜-inch hem, being sure to catch all ten ties.

Pull the ties up, so that they are facing away from the curtain panel, and topstitch all the way across. Repeat steps for the other curtain panel.

Search online for "vintage grain sack" to get some stripe pattern and color ideas. Red, tan, blue, and black are some historically accurate colors to choose for your stripes.

HOW TO MAKE FAUX GRAIN-SACK FABRIC

I love the simple stripe pattern and weathered vintage appeal of grain-sack fabric in my farmhouse. I sometimes come across gorgeous textiles from antique shops that are in great condition, but many times they have stains and holes. You can purchase reproduction grain-sack fabric, or try your hand at painting your own. All it takes is a little craft paint, tape, and drop cloth to make fabric reminiscent of gorgeous vintage grain sack. Use it to make table runners, pillow covers, tote bags, Christmas stockings, and tea towels.

MATERIALS

Canvas drop cloth
Craft paint
Craft paintbrush
Painter's tape
Steel wool

INSTRUCTIONS

Cut the drop cloth out for the project you want to make. You could make up several yards of faux drop-cloth fabric for a project at a future date, but it is much less work if you are only painting just enough for your project.

Use painter's tape to make one of the many grain-sack stripe patterns from long ago. I went with several different patterns and stripe widths.

Apply craft paint between the tape with a dry craft paintbrush. The goal is to make the stripes a little wispy and not so solid.

Once the stripe is dry, scratch it up a bit with something abrasive, like steel wool. This will give it the vintage grain-sack look.

GRAIN-SACK TABLE RUNNER

Reproduction grain-sack fabric has a tendency to shrink when washed. If you cut straight into a fresh bolt of fabric and create a custom-length runner for your table, you may find yourself a bit dismayed the first time a little mustard stain sends it to the wash, never to return the same size again. Don't ask me how many times it took me to learn this lesson. I like to wash my fabric on hot and hang it to dry before working with it. You can also make your own faux grain-sack fabric (see page 63).

MATERIALS

2-plus yards reproduction (or hand-painted) grain-sack fabric (more depending on the table size)

1 spool of coordinating thread

INSTRUCTIONS

Wash and dry the grain-sack fabric.

Measure your table.

Cut out the grain-sack fabric. Take the length of your table and add several inches for an overhang. For a small table, like my 4-foot coffee table, I prefer the runner to hang 6 inches over both edges. For larger tables, like my 8-foot dining-room table, I prefer the runner to hang 12 inches over both edges. You also need to add an inch to each side for the hem allowance.

For the width of the runner, I like a finished width of 14 inches for smaller tables and 28 inches for larger tables. Again, add 2 inches to the width for hem allowance.

Press all four sides over ½ inch and then another ½ inch toward the wrong side of the fabric. Sew a ⅜-inch hem all the way around, making sure to back- and forward-stitch at the beginning and end.

SAMPLE TABLE RUNNER PATTERN SIZES

Small Table (4 feet): 16 inches wide by 62 inches long (cut one)

Large Table (8 feet): 30 inches wide by 122 inches long (cut one)

FAUX TICKING-STRIPE SHEETS

I adapted these plain white sheets to decorate my farmhouse bedroom last summer. I love the way a turned-back top sheet can add a bit of color and pattern to a room while still coordinating with the throw pillows and pillowcases on the bed. I thought a touch of blue ticking stripe would be beautiful, but I already had a set of plain white sheets that I wasn't ready to part with for the season. By adding a band of fabric to the top, I was able to fake the look without buying all-new sheets.

MATERIALS

1½ yards light- to medium-weight fabric, such as cotton or linen

Top sheet

MEASURE, MARK, AND CUT

20 inches long by 90½ inches wide (cut one)

INSTRUCTIONS

My top sheet is 88½ inches wide, so to ensure that I had enough space on each side to hem the raw edges, I made my fabric piece 90½ inches. (The standard queen sheet is usually about 90 inches wide, but they can vary slightly, so make sure to check the width of yours first. Add 2 inches to that measurement for hem allowance, to determine the width.) Almost no fabric is 90 inches wide, so you may need to join two pieces together with a seam in the middle to reach the 90½ inches width.

Sew the band on. Line the fabric band up with the top of the top sheet, with right sides together, leaving a 1-inch

MORE TIPS FOR GIVING YOUR TOP SHEET A LITTLE MAKEOVER

- Use a vintage floral for spring. When you find a beautiful vintage sheet that is in less-than-perfect condition, cut the top portion off and sew it to your favorite comfy sheet you already own.

- Near the top hem of the fabric band, add a coordinating ruffle. This would look especially lovely in a little girl's room.

- You can have "linen" sheets without the expense by adding your favorite shade of washed linen to the top of a plain old cotton sheet.

- Add some antique lace edging or crochet vintage trim to the top hem of a sheet. You could do this one with or without sewing on a different fabric band.

overhang on each side. Pin in place. Sew top sheet to the fabric band with a ½-inch seam. Serge or zigzag-stitch the seam to finish off the raw edges.

Hem the fabric band. Fold and press the 1-inch overhang on each side of the fabric band, over ½ inch and then another ½ inch, to hide the raw edges inside. Sew the side hems down with a ⅜-inch hem. Fold and press the top of the fabric band over 1 inch and then another 1 inch, to hide the raw edges inside. Sew the top hem down with a ⅞-inch hem.

LINEN-WRAPPED BALLS

Yield: Five linen-wrapped balls

Unfussy and super easy to make, linen-wrapped balls are a beautiful addition to an antique iron-stone bowl or wicker basket. Use them to add a little color to built-ins, bookshelves, and mantles, or as a pretty coffee-table display. They're reminiscent of old country rag balls, but the linen adds a soft stonewashed look.

MATERIALS

Several strips of linen fabric (Fabrics that have the appearance of linen, like linen blends, drop cloth, and grain sack, are also good choices.)
Five 3-inch Styrofoam balls
Hot glue

INSTRUCTIONS

Cut several 1-inch-wide strips of linen fabric, each one at least 10 inches in length. (Longer length means you won't have to piece together as many strips to cover the ball.) A 10-inch length ensures that it will go around the ball at least a couple of times.

Put a small dab of hot glue at the end of one linen strip. Press it on the Styrofoam ball.

Begin wrapping the linen around the ball in kind of a crisscross fashion, adding hot glue as you go.

When you come to the end of one strip, hot-glue on another, and continue wrapping until the entire ball is covered.

Repeat for the other four balls.

Hot-glue a small piece of jute string to the top to turn these linen-wrapped balls into easy-to-make Christmas ornaments!

HOW TO DYE DROP CLOTH

I remember the first time it occurred to me that my favorite cheap fabric could become any color I wanted it to be. Since then, I have experimented with dyeing drop cloth in various shades of blue, black, gray, and tan. The results can be unpredictable, but I have yet to come across an end product I haven't loved.

Experiment with the amount of dye you add to the water, and the length of time the fabric is submerged, until you get a color you are happy with. If you're like me, you'll just wing it and hope for the best. I have never ended up with fabric I couldn't use. For the particular swatches in the photo, I filled my top-loading washer to the medium level (plus a few pots of boiling water) and used one 8-ounce container of dye. I added about a quarter cup of sea salt and allowed the swatch to soak in the water for 30 minutes, before finishing out the cycle and hanging to dry.

MATERIALS

100 percent cotton canvas drop cloth (synthetic blends will require a dye specifically made for synthetic fibers)
Liquid fabric dye
Boiling water
Sea salt

INSTRUCTIONS

Fill the washer with hot water and a few pots of boiling water. Add fabric dye and ½ cup sea salt. Follow the package instructions for the amount of dye to add. Allow the machine to agitate for a few minutes to incorporate the dye. Add the drop cloth to the dye water. Allow the machine to agitate for a few more minutes to get the fabric fully submerged in the dye/salt water.

TIPS FOR SUCCESSFUL FABRIC DYING

- Don't overcrowd the washer. If you purchase a 9-by-12-foot drop cloth, like I often do, divide it in half and dye it in two separate batches.

- Cotton and linen dye best in extra hot water, while wool does better in warm water.

- Sea salt helps the dye saturation in linen and cotton. For wool, distilled white vinegar is preferable.

- If you do not have a top-loading washer, use a stainless-steel bucket or sink and a large spoon for the dye bath.

- If you desire very dark, saturated colors, use double the recommended amount of dye and salt, and increase the soaking time. Consider using the stovetop method, where you actually dye the fabric in boiling water in a stainless-steel pot, right on the stove.

Let the drop cloth soak in the dye for about 30 minutes, or as long as desired. A longer soak will give a higher dye saturation. It is difficult to truly know the color you are getting until the fabric dries, but you can use stainless-steel tongs to pull the fabric out of the water to check the color. Finish the washer cycle, with one extra rinse. Hang the dyed drop cloth to dry.

(**Note:** If you need to dye several drop cloths the exact same color—say, for a colored slipcover or several panels of matching curtains—there are a few tricks to ensure that they will be consistent. Divide the fabric in equal parts before washing, and fill the washer to the same level each time; likewise, make sure to add the exact same portion of dye, salt, and boiling water to each batch. Set a timer to ensure they are submerged for the same amount of time in the dye water.)

FARMHOUSE-STYLE SHELF DISPLAYS

Creating farmhouse-style shelf displays can be overwhelming. Whether it's one small kitchen shelf or floor-to-ceiling built-ins, the challenge is making something fresh and beautiful that isn't too cluttered, and the key is patience, trial, and error. Place something up there, step back, examine, move it, step back, and repeat. I love changing my shelves up for the seasons with pumpkins in the fall, and greenery and stockings in the winter months. Family photos and books bring in the coziness and personalization. Here are other tips:

- Select something large to anchor the bottom of the shelves. I place baskets all along the bottom row of our custom built-in shelving. They are also great for storage!

- Keep shelves balanced with pieces of similar shapes and sizes on opposite sides.

- Focus on natural textures and neutral colors. I had color photographs in my frames, and they were throwing off the whole color scheme. I swapped them out for black-and-white photographs to improve the flow.

- Use antiques sparingly. Shelves can start to look tacky if you throw in too many random pieces from garage sales and antique shops. Instead, focus on timeless pieces such as ironstone, crocks, and wooden boxes.

- Bring in something fresh. Our built-in shelves never look quite complete without fresh flowers, potted plants, pumpkins, or greenery.

- Use different heights and shapes on each shelf. For example, I paired a large ironstone pitcher next to a small one.

- Layers make shelves look more interesting and cozy. I put a potted plant and ironstone pitcher in front of a wooden box. I also created layers with my ironstone soup tureen and blue plate.

- Add in a little color. My favorite way to do this is with fresh flowers and plants. I also like to add in pieces from my blue ironstone collection.

- Incorporate a vintage mirror.

CHAPTER 3

COLLECTING ANTIQUES AND VINTAGE FINDS

IF I COULD DREAM UP MY PERFECT DAY, it would involve loading up my husband and kids in the van and setting out to find every antiques shop within a 30-mile radius. Coffee in hand, I'd sift through pottery, textiles, wooden crates, ironstone, and baskets.

I love looking at my newfound treasures with an eye toward how I can repurpose them into something useful and beautiful for our home. It might be a pillow cover from a vintage grain sack, a child's apron from an embroidered napkin, or hand-poured candles in old crocks and jars.

My keys to collecting are to pay a little extra for quality, and to keep your own personal style or palette in mind. When I first started collecting, I'd bring home every $2 white pitcher I laid eyes on. These days I know it is better to spend $20 on a vintage ironstone pitcher with a beautiful patina than ten cheap pieces devoid of character.

Don't be afraid of the imperfections you're likely to find in antique pieces. As long as they are solid, a little ding here or chipped paint there only adds more character and charm. Creating coziness and personality in a home is a slow process of finding pieces you love and crafting things with your own two hands. It can't be done with one quick shopping spree at the home decor store. Plan to spend years and enjoy the process along the way.

PLATE GALLERY WALL

Vintage plates are too pretty to hide away in a cabinet, and many times are too chipped to actually serve a meal on. I love them in a farmhouse because they are beautiful in an ordinary and practical way. I recently came across an entire box of flow blue English china and snapped it right up for my first plate gallery wall in our new farmhouse.

MATERIALS

Antique plates

Plate hangers

Picture-hanging hooks

INSTRUCTIONS

As with any DIY project, there is the "this has to be done perfectly type-A way," and then there is the "slap it up and hope for the best because my kids are going to wake up any minute" method. Yours truly falls into the latter category every single time, but I have written enough posts on the Internet and received enough comments to know that not everyone does things like me.

To arrange the plates the "proper" way, cut a piece of poster paper, wrapping paper, or newspaper to the size of the wall area you want to cover with a plate arrangement. Arrange your plates exactly as you want them on the paper, and trace around each plate. This

PLATE HANGER OPTIONS

Adhesive disc hangers: One type is an adhesive disc that attaches to the back of the plate. They are completely invisible from the back of the plate and super easy to use, but they are also easily knocked off the walls by little hands (ask me how I know), and the plates will always have something stuck to the back, so grabbing them down for a dinner party isn't feasible.

Metal plate hangers: These hangers essentially hook around the front of the plate in four areas. These are a bit safer for precious china, but the hooks are slightly visible from the front. Vinyl-coated versions can be a bit pricier, but they protect your plates from getting scratched. I would suggest displaying your inexpensive antique finds in plate gallery walls, and saving the priceless family heirlooms for the inside of a more-secure hutch or cabinet.

will serve as a plate placement guide, so you can be sure you get them up precisely as you planned.

To arrange the plates the "wing it" way, place them how you like them on the floor and then snap a picture with your smartphone to help you remember approximately where they should go.

To hang the plates the "proper" way, measure the distance from the top of the plate to the area on the back where it will hook into the nail or picture hanger. Measure and mark where the nail hole will go on each of the plate outlines. Tape the large template onto the wall and nail the picture-hanging hooks straight through the paper. Rip the paper down, and hang your plates on the hooks.

To hang the plates the "wing it" way, start by nailing a picture-hanging hook in the wall and hanging the first plate, around where you want the middle of the arrangement to go. Work outward from the middle, eyeballing the placement as you go.

TIPS FOR DISPLAYING
ANTIQUE CHINA

- **Think beyond the plate:** Ironstone tureen lids, scalloped-edge bowls, and platters look great mixed in an antique china gallery wall.

- **Vary the sizes and colors:** Collections with a mix of small, medium, and large plates in various vintage hues are interesting to look at.

- **Keep it simple:** If you're not sure where to start, try hanging three monochromatic plates in a straight line on either side of a window.

KIDS' APRON FROM VINTAGE RUNNER

When perusing local thrift shops and antiques malls, I try to keep a creative eye out for possible ways to repurpose items. One thing I spot time and time again is linens of all varieties, from lace napkins and floral tablecloths to handmade aprons and pretty sheets. I've made summer pajamas for my girls from floral sheets, pillows from old grain sacks, and a quirky dress from vintage floral drapes. Recently I found a detailed cross-stitch table scarf for only three dollars. I thought about the amount of time that someone in the past spent tediously placing each delicate thread. The entire thing had a hand-stitched crochet trim border. Far be it from me to pass on something so beautiful and time-consuming! Though I didn't have a table to bring it home to, I knew it could be transformed into two pretty aprons for my girls.

Even if you don't know exactly how you will repurpose a vintage linen right away, bring it home to your stash for when inspiration strikes. I promise you will never find fabrics as beautiful at the big-box craft stores.

MATERIALS

Vintage textiles

Linen fabric for the strap

> Want to show off your handmade items in more places than your kitchen? Sew a pretty apron like this straight into the hemline of a dress. It adds a fun and whimsical detail that will put a smile on your little girl's face. Check out my Bow-in-the-Back Summer Dress tutorial on farmhouseonboone .com to get some ideas.

INSTRUCTIONS

Cut a long strip of linen 72 inches by 4 inches. Cut the main apron piece from your vintage material. Ideally the finished apron will be about 18 inches wide and 12 to 15 inches long. The table scarf that I made my aprons from was already finished around the outside, so I did not need to account for a hem. If yours is not, or you are cutting from a large sheet or tablecloth, add 1 inch to the sides and bottom.

So, for example, if you are cutting from a large sheet, cut a piece 15 inches by 20 inches for the main apron piece. Hem the two sides and bottom of the main apron piece (if the sides are not already finished). To do this, press the raw edge ½ inch, and then another ½ inch, to the wrong side of the fabric. Sew all the way around the three sides. You can leave the top unfinished, because it will be covered by the linen apron strap.

With your machine's stitch length set as high as it will go, add a gathering stitch to the top of the main apron piece. Pull the gathering strings gently until the top is about 12 inches wide. *(Figure 1)*

Press both long sides of the linen strap piece ½ inch toward the wrong side of the fabric. Fold the whole linen piece in half, so that the two pressed edges line up and no raw edges are showing. Press in place. *(Figure 2)*

Center the main apron piece on the strap, and sandwich the top (gathered) edge of the main apron piece in between. *(Figure 3)*

Pin it in place and sew all the way around the linen strap, with a very narrow top-stitch. Make sure to back- and forward-stitch at the beginning and end. *(Figure 4)*

Put that pretty thing on your little girl, and enjoy!

Figure 1

Figure 3

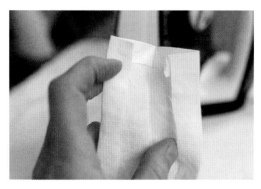

Figure 2

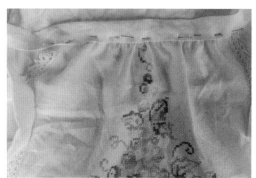

Figure 4

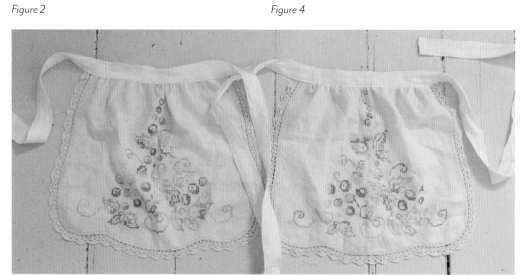

CROCHET TABLE-TOPPER STOOL MAKEOVER

When I came across a crochet vintage table topper for five bucks at one of my favorite local antiques shops, I knew it was coming home with me. With its pretty cream color, soft vintage drape, and all that detailed handiwork, it just belonged in the farmhouse. Though putting a lace crochet doily on a table looks a little too much like my grandmother's house, I knew I could repurpose it into something beautiful. I had an old stool that I'd also snagged inexpensively, and thought my two thrifty finds were meant to be together. I removed the seat and covered the old vinyl top with my newly acquired crochet doily. The stool is still a little beat-up, with scuffs and paint chips, but the lovely crochet detail on the top makes it a pretty addition to any room in our home.

MATERIALS

An old upholstered stool or bench

Vintage linens (crochet table topper, old grain sack, vintage sheets)

White fabric (linen, drop cloth, or cotton)

INSTRUCTIONS

Turn the stool over and remove the top with the appropriate screwdriver, either a Phillips-head or a flathead. Save the screws, because you will need them to attach the seat again later.

If you are using crochet or lace, you will want to cover the seat of the stool first with a coordinating piece of fabric. I used white, so that no dark colors would peek through the doily holes. (If you are using something that is not see-through, such as a tablecloth, grain sack, or sheets, you can skip this step.) Cut the piece of fabric so that it is large enough to cover the stool top and reach underneath it. Cutting it too large is better than too small, because you can always trim it later.

Lay the stool seat facedown on the fabric. Starting on one long side, pull the fabric to the bottom of the seat and staple it in place. Do the same on the other long side, pulling it taut and stapling in place. Repeat with the two short sides. Wrap the remaining fabric around the corners and staple in place.

Attach the vintage linens exactly the same way you attached the fabric. If you are using something stretchy, like my crochet doily, don't pull it as taut; you don't want to stretch it out and make the holes larger.

With the seat still turned over, trim the excess fabric all the way around, about 1 inch from the staples. Turn the stool over and reattach the seat with the screws you removed earlier.

DUVET FROM VINTAGE SHEETS

Vintage sheets provide some of my favorite fabric to work with. Many times a portion of the fabric is stained or damaged, but I can cut around those areas to create tea towels, dresses, curtains, and pillowcases. Sometimes, though, I find the most beautiful vintage sheets that have been untouched and carefully stored away in their original packaging. They are too nice to cut up and too pretty to hide beneath a comforter. When I find two such coordinating sheets, a reversible duvet cover is in order. This is easy to make, and rescues beautiful sheets from a hidden fate.

MATERIALS

Two full- or queen-size vintage sheets
Twin or full duvet comforter

Figure 1

Figure 2

INSTRUCTIONS

Cut the large top hem, and about ½ inch of fabric below it, off of one of the sheets. Set aside. (*Figure 1*)

Lay the same vintage sheet on the floor, and lay the comforter insert that you plan to use on top of it. Leaving about 6 inches on all four sides of the insert, cut any excess fabric from the sheet. Cut the other vintage sheet to the same size. Leave the smaller sheet hem on one short side in place. This is a way to skip having to put a top hem back in the duvet later! (For reference, I made a twin duvet and cut my sheets to 95 inches long by 74 inches wide.) This is a little bigger than a standard twin duvet, but I wanted to be able to fold back the top and show off that pretty blue fabric on the back.

For the ties, cut twelve strips of fabric 16 inches long by 2½ inches wide. (I just used the long strip that I cut off of one of my sheets in the first step.) On one short end of a tie piece, press over ½ inch toward the wrong side of the fabric. Fold the two long edges in, so that they meet in the middle. (*Figure 2*)

Then fold the tie in half lengthwise. Topstitch all along the two long sides and the folded short side, with a very narrow seam. (This is my quick and easy way to make ties, but you can also use the safety-pin method I used in the Tie-Top Linen Curtains project on page 61.) Repeat to finish off the other eleven tie pieces. (*Figure 3*)

Figure 3

Figure 4

Take the large hem that you cut off of one of the sheets in the first step and line it back up with the top of the sheet, with right sides together. (You're basically going to be attaching it on like it was before, only with the ties sandwiched between.) Starting at one end, put the unfinished edge of one of the ties between the sheet hem and the main sheet piece. Pin it in place. *(Figure 4)*

Repeat with five more ties, evenly spacing them out along the top of the duvet. There will be six ties total in this side of the duvet. The large top hem will create a pocket for the duvet insert to rest inside. Take the pocket and fold it to the wrong side of the sheet. Press the seam flat and topstitch it down, with a narrow seam at the top. *(Figure 5)*

With right sides together, line up the front duvet piece with the back duvet piece on all four sides. Make sure that the hem you left in place in the first step is at the top. With a ½-inch seam, sew the two sheets together around the bottom and the two long sides. Leave the top open. Make sure to back- and forward-stitch at the beginning and end. Finish the raw edges off with a serger or zigzag stitch. Turn the duvet cover right side out.

Take the remaining six ties and sew them along the top of the other sheet (I like to do this step after sewing the two sheets together, so that I can see where the ties from the first sheet hit the second sheet, and easily line them up as I go). Instead of removing the hem, like I did with the insert pocket on the first sheet, I just folded the raw edge of each tie under and sewed them on individually. *(Figure 6)*

(**Optional:** To keep the duvet insert in place, you can make eight additional ties and sew two in each inside corner. Stuff the insert inside your duvet and secure each corner with the ties. Tie the top ties in bows to keep the duvet closed.)

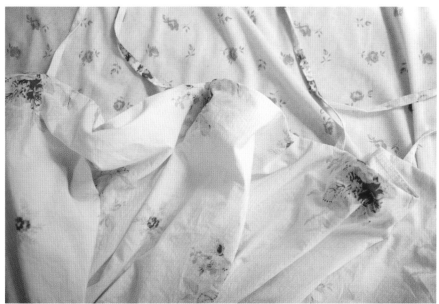

Figure 5

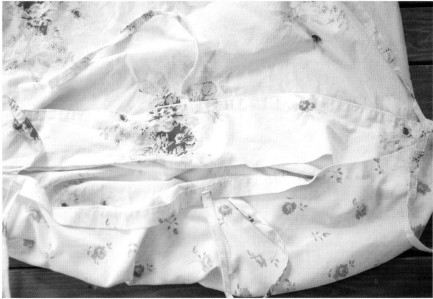

Figure 6

LINEN BENCH SLIPCOVER

Most of the time the antique furniture I come across when I'm out thrifting needs some level of revamping to fit into my simple farmhouse aesthetic. The most important consideration is that the piece is sturdy and has a shape I like. This is what the design experts call "good bones." With benches, chairs, and stools, the refinishing options are usually reupholstering or slipcovering. Though I've done both, this mom of six far and away prefers one over the other.

Imagine this scenario: A mud-puddle-splashing, frozen-blueberry-eating toddler comes barreling into the living room with no regard for the furnishings. Do you a) want something that you can remove and throw in the wash, or b) something that has been permanently affixed to the piece with nails and glue? I can assure you that the former, even if it is all white, fresh, and beautiful, is preferable to the latter.

I've done it myself—reupholstered a gorgeous antique chair with vintage ticking fabric. I've also slipcovered two wingbacks with bleached-white fabric. Guess which item met its fate at a Goodwill drop-off less than a year after entering our home, and which ones we still sit on today?

I'm a big fan of slipcovering. Though tackling a fitted wingback or couch is a more-advanced sewing practice, a simple bench slipcover can be achieved by beginners.

MATERIALS

Linen or linen/cotton blend fabric (The amount will depend on the size of your bench. For my small bench, I was able to use about a yard and a half of leftover linen I had from another project.)

INSTRUCTIONS

For the main piece, cut a large linen rectangle that will hang over each edge about 5 inches. My bench is 23 inches long by 14 inches wide, so I cut my main piece 33 inches long by 24 inches wide. *(Figure 1)*

For the ties, cut four strips 4½ inches wide. The length of the ties will depend on the width of your bench. For my 14-inch-wide bench, my tie pieces were 16 inches long by 4½ inches wide. This allows them to overlap and create a tie at the ends of the bench.

For the ruffle piece, measure the diameter of your bench and multiply it by 1½ to get the length. The width of the ruffle is 4½ inches. My bench is 78 inches around, so my ruffle needed to be about 117 inches long by 4½ inches wide.

Fold one tie piece in half, with right sides together. Sew down the long side and one short side, creating a curve toward the top. The curve is optional, but it does create a pretty detail in the tie. Trim the excess fabric around the curve, being careful not to cut into your stitching. Use your fingers to push the tie pieces right side out. Center the seam in the middle and press flat. Topstitch all the way around the tie. Repeat with the other three tie pieces. *(Figure 2)*

Sew the two short ends of the ruffle piece together, with right sides facing. Sew a hem all the way around the bottom of the ruffle piece by pressing the raw edge over ½ inch and then another ½ inch, and sewing in place. Put a gathering stitch in the unfinished top edge of the ruffle piece. I like to do several gathering stitches on a long piece like this, to ensure that I don't break any strings.

Place the main piece on top of the bench. On one corner, fold the fabric so that it fits snugly on the bench. Place the unfinished short edge of one tie piece inside the fold and pin in place. *(Figure 3)* Make sure the seam is facing the bench, so that the pretty edge of the tie faces up. Repeat for the other three corners. Adjust the folds until they all rest evenly on the corners and look the same length.

Figure 1

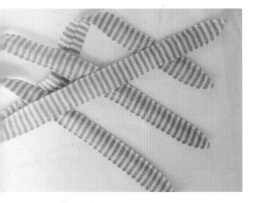

Figure 2

Once everything is all even, remove the snug slipcover from the bench and sew down the four corners, making sure to catch all four ties.

Put the slipcover back on the bench and trim all the way around until it hangs down evenly on all sides. Mine hangs down 3¼ inches at this point.

Pull the gathering strings on the ruffle piece, until the size meets the size of the bottom of the slipcover. Pin it on with right sides together, and sew all the way around with a ½-inch seam.

Finish the raw edge with a zigzag stitch or serger.

Figure 3

LAVENDER ORANGE CANDLES
IN ANTIQUE POTTERY

This project combines two of my favorite things: beautiful antiques and simple, all-natural ingredients. Candles can be made in nearly any pottery that has a sufficient opening at the top and is deep enough to hold wax. Ironstone bowls, small crocks, vintage tin measuring cups, and Mason jars with wire bails all work beautifully. They make excellent gifts, so keep your eye out for those perfect candle vessels all year long, with your Christmas gift list in mind.

I made these with lavender and orange essential oils, but you can experiment with other scent combinations for your own homemade candles. One of my favorite winter scents is cinnamon and clove. You can smell them from across the room! Of course, essential oils are completely optional, but they do lend a lovely scent to the already-sweet-smelling beeswax.

I normally use my top-notch, high-quality essential oils for everything in my home, but for candles I am willing to make an exception. It takes a huge amount to scent candles, so I just grab some cheap oils from a bulk soap-making shop.

MATERIALS

A few small vintage candle vessels

1 pound beeswax pellets, or wax from a local beekeeper, cut into large pieces

1 teaspoon lavender essential oil

1 teaspoon orange essential oil

Braided candlewick

Hot glue

Dowel rod

INSTRUCTIONS

Melt the beeswax in a double boiler or a glass bowl over a small pot of boiling water. Add the essential oils.

Cut a 12-inch length of candlewicking. Tie a couple of knots in the bottom of the wicking to create surface area to secure the wicks to the vessel.

Add a little hot glue to the knotted area and press it down on the bottom of the vessel, making sure it is centered. Pull the wicking up and wrap it several times around a dowel rod. (You can also use a pencil; this is just to keep the top of the wick out of the wax while pouring.)

Pour the melted beeswax in the jar, stopping before you reach the dowel rod. Work quickly, because the wax will begin to harden right away.

When the beeswax is fully hardened, trim the wicks to about ¼ inch in length.

VINTAGE GRAIN-SACK PILLOW COVER

Vintage grain sacks make the perfect fabric for a simple decorative throw pillow. With minimal sewing, this project comes together in minutes. I love layering them on the bed with a few Euro shams, or on the couch for a special farmhouse touch. They also look pretty stuffed in a wicker basket with a cozy throw blanket.

When you're selecting vintage materials for this project, look for a grain sack that has minimal stains and rips. Usually old sacks can't handle heavy washes, so getting tough stains out can be tricky. Crochet trim is my favorite to work with, but you can also use lace or eyelet.

MATERIALS

Vintage grain sack

Extra-wide double-fold bias tape

Vintage crochet trim

INSTRUCTIONS

To make the ties, cut two 18-inch-long pieces of bias tape. Take one of your pieces of bias tape and fold one end under. Sew the folded end in place, and then all the way down the open (non-folded) side of the bias tape. Repeat with the other 18-inch piece of bias tape.

To finish off the open end of the grain sack, place the trim just under the top edge of the open end of the grain sack, and pin in place. Make sure to overlap it where the two ends meet.

Sew close to the edge, nearly all the way around, making sure to stop just before you reach the overlapping ends. Sew the ends with right sides together, and cut off any excess. Sew the finished overlapping ends to the grain sack with a narrow seam.

Find the center of the pillow cover opening by folding it in half and marking it with a straight pin. Add a matching pin on the other side. Tuck the unfinished edge of one bias-tape tie under, and pin it to the center on one side of the opening. Repeat with the other tie on the other side. Sew both ties in place.

I decided to do something a little different for my pillow cover, adding ties and trim to both ends. If you choose to do this step, use sharp scissors to cut closely to the finished end of the grain sack. Serge or zigzag-stitch around the unfinished end. Fold the unfinished edge toward the inside of the grain sack, about ½ inch. Press and stitch with a narrow hem. Add the trim and bias tape to the opening.

PILLOWCASE WITH HEIRLOOM TRIM

As a kid, I sewed a few "official" things with patterns to show in the exhibit hall at the county fair, but for the most part I just played around with fabric and the sewing machine. Let's just say it was a few years before I made something I could actually wear out in public.

The one thing I made early on that actually turned out every time was a pillowcase. If you are a beginner, pillowcases really are the easiest thing to sew; they're just rectangles and straight stitches. When my girls were little, I sewed them with layers of ruffles and lace trims to dress up their plain white bedding.

The options for customizing them are endless, but the basic tutorial is easy and quick. The fun thing is, you need exactly 1 yard of fabric for this project, with nothing left over.

For this one, I added some beautiful crochet trim that I snagged for cheap at a thrift shop, but you can substitute some eyelet, or just leave it out altogether!

MATERIALS

1 yard light- to medium-weight 44-inch-wide fabric, like linen, cotton, or a linen/cotton blend

Crochet trim (optional)

MEASURE, MARK, AND CUT

Main piece, 27 inches by 44 inches

Band at the top, 10 inches by 44 inches

Crochet trim, 44 inches long

INSTRUCTIONS

You will use the entire width of the fabric, but you want to make sure to cut the selvage (i.e., edge) of both pieces.

Press the 10-by-44-inch piece in half lengthwise down the center. Open the band piece back up and lay it out, with the right side of the fabric facing up. Lay the main piece, with the right side of the fabric also laying up, on top of the band piece, with the raw edges lined up. Lastly, line the vintage trim up along the top with the raw edges of the main piece and band piece. It is basically a band piece / main piece / trim sandwich at this point! *(Figure 1)*

Roll the main piece up toward the top like a burrito. This will expose the 10-inch band piece below it. Fold the band piece up over the main piece, along the line that you originally pressed, and line up the raw edge with the other raw edges at the top. Pin the four layers at the top together, and stitch with a ¼-inch seam. *(Figure 2)* Pull the tube right side out.

Figure 1

IDEAS FOR CUSTOMIZING YOUR PILLOWCASES

- Make the top band in a coordinating color. A soft floral next to a light blue linen with lace trim sandwiched between would look beautiful.

- Add a few layers of pink gingham ruffles to the top of a girly pillowcase made from Amy Butler's "pink and ivory floating buds" quilting fabric. (I wish I had a picture of the one I made for my daughter before she defaced it with a permanent marker at age two.)

- Instead of sandwiching crochet trim in between the main piece and band piece, fold a 2-inch-wide coordinating piece of cotton fabric and add it instead.

Figure 2

At this point, you will have the top all nicely finished, with the raw edges hidden inside. To complete the pillowcase, fold it in half lengthwise with right sides together, and stitch down the long open side and the bottom with a ½-inch seam. Finish the seam with a serger or a zigzag stitch. Turn the pillowcase right side out.

GIRLS' PAJAMAS FROM VINTAGE SHEETS

I first made these pajamas for my girls a few summers ago when I came across some vintage sheets in excellent condition, just begging for a repurposing project. I loved the light and airy pattern of the faded florals and thought they would be perfect for summer PJ sets. I never like to sew anything super complicated, so I decided to make easy elastic shorts and a simple pillowcase-style top.

MATERIALS

1 vintage flat sheet

¼-inch elastic

1-inch elastic

¼-inch bias tape

MEASURE, MARK, AND CUT

Sizes 2–4: Top, 15 inches long by 16 inches wide (cut two); bias tape straps, 15 inches long (cut two); neck elastic, 5 inches (cut one); waistband elastic, 22 inches (cut one)

Sizes 4–6: Top, 17 inches long by 18 inches wide (cut two); bias tape straps, 16 inches long (cut two); neck elastic, 6 inches (cut one); waistband elastic, 24 inches (cut one)

Sizes 6–8: Top, 19 inches long by 20 inches wide (cut two); bias tape straps, 17 inches long (cut two); neck elastic, 7 inches (cut one); waistband elastic, 26 inches (cut one)

Sizes 8–10: Top, 21 inches long by 22 inches wide (cut two); bias tape straps, 18 inches long (cut two); neck elastic, 8 inches (cut one); waistband elastic, 28 inches (cut one)

INSTRUCTIONS

Measure, mark, and cut two rectangular pieces, for the pajama top, from the cut list.

To create the armhole pattern, take a small piece of fabric or paper and cut out a 3-inch by 4-inch square, and round off the bottom right corner. Fold each top piece in half (horizontally) and use your pattern to cut out notches for the armholes on the top side, opposite the fold.

Figure 1

Figure 2

Figure 3

Line the two top pieces up, with the right sides together, and pin along the sides. Sew the sides with a ½-inch seam. Press the top edge of the front shirt piece down ½ inch and then another ½ inch, hiding the raw edge inside, to create the elastic casing. Sew the hem in place.

Add a safety pin to the end of a piece of ¼-inch elastic, using the neck elastic measurements from the cut list. Push the elastic through the casing of the front and sew it in place on both sides of the casing. Repeat for the back top piece.

For the straps, cut two pieces of double-fold bias tape from the cut list measurements.

Starting at the side seam of the top, fold the bias tape in half and sandwich the raw edge of the top inside. Pin it in place. Next, pin the other side of the strap in place at the seam, overlapping the first. Sew all the way around the strap, making sure to catch all the layers of the bias tape and the armhole in between.

Next, it is time to make the shorts. I already confessed that I am not a pattern user. Anytime I am making things for my kids, I go to their closet and pull out a dress or pants that currently fit them and steal measurements from there.

I measure the length of the elastic in a waistband, the length of the hemlines, the width of the bodice and length of sleeves. No need to search the internet for standard measurements. Just go find all the info you need right in your child's closet. The same goes for the shape of shorts and tops. I pulled a pair of pajama pants out my daughter's drawer and used it for the pattern piece for the shorts. I simply folded it in half and cut around it, leaving room for the seams (about three-quarters of an inch) and extra space at the top (about 3 inches) for the elastic waistband.

Cut four pieces (two for the front and two for the back). Make sure that you have two facing one way and two facing the other, so cut your fabric right side up to cut two and then the wrong side up to cut the other two. Pin and sew, with right sides together and a ½-inch seam, down the center seem. This will create one piece for the front and one piece for the back.

Line up the front and back short pieces, with right sides together, and sew down the sides with a ½-inch seam. Next, sew around the crotch, making sure to line up the front center seam to the back center seam.

To make the waistband elastic casing, press the top down 1½ inches and then another 1½ inches, hiding the raw edges inside. Sew the waistband almost all the way around, leaving a 1-inch opening to push the elastic through.

Cut a piece of 1-inch elastic from the cut list. Push the elastic all the way through until it meets up with the other end at the opening. Overlap the ends, being careful that you don't have them twisted. Sew the ends to each other with several back and forward stitches. Sew up the 1-inch spot that you left open to pull the elastic through.

TIPS TO JAZZ UP THE JAMMIES

For a pop of color in the straps, buy bias tape in a color other than white. I like the vintage feel of neutrals, but I also think it would be fun to use blue, pink, or green for the straps.

Add eyelets, pom-pom trim, or lace to the bottom of the finished pajama top and shorts. Just search vintage trims online and behold the possibilities.

Try adding elastic only through the back of the top, and add eyelet and bias tape to the front.

CHAPTER 4

NATURAL HANDMADE BODY

ALMOST TEN YEARS AGO when I became a new mom, I started looking long and hard at the products I was going to be putting on my precious newborn. It didn't take a whole lot of digging to find out that conventional body products weren't developed with wellness in mind. They were filled with a whole lot of junk and words I couldn't pronounce.

Turns out it's simple to make healing salves and balms, lotions, toothpaste, and other basic body products at home. I find myself using the same ingredients, like beeswax, coconut oil, essential oils, and herbs, again and again to make these products for my family. A couple extra ingredients turn my basic body butter into sunscreen. Tweaking my sunscreen a touch makes the best diaper-rash cream I've ever used to doctor up many a sore bottom. With a small arsenal in your home apothecary, you can treat many of the minor aches and irritations that come your way.

Nearly all of my go-to natural body-care products use a double boiler, so the most efficient way to get all the lotion, lip balm, deodorant, soap, and salve that your family needs is to make them at the same time. Devote one day a month—or if you're really ambitious, one day a year—to mussing up the kitchen and dragging out every last bit of beeswax, shea butter, and coconut oil you have to knock it out in bulk.

OATMEAL AND HONEY SOAP
WITH CALENDULA

These beautiful soap bars are all natural and healthy for the skin. Wrapped with a jute string or a strip of linen, they make the perfect gift. Melt-and-pour soap bases are great when you want that homespun feel but don't want to mess with lye and all the safety gear and precision that comes with it. You can simply cut an all-natural soap base into cubes, melt it down, and add in whatever herbs, essential oils, and natural colorings suit your fancy.

A note about the ingredients: Oatmeal acts as an all-natural exfoliant. It also has antimicrobial properties and is an excellent moisturizer. The age-old practice of soothing oatmeal baths is rooted in the fact that oatmeal is indeed great for the skin! Honey is naturally antibacterial and moisturizing. It is chock-full of antioxidants and enzymes that nourish the skin. Calendula has skin-healing properties and looks beautiful in the finished soap. I love something that has a practical use but also looks pretty in my home.

INGREDIENTS

**2 pounds melt-and-pour soap base
(I use a goat's milk base, but shea
butter is also a great option.)**

½ cup dried calendula

**2 tablespoons oatmeal, pulsed in a
blender until it is in powder form (I
just use my coffee grinder for this.)**

2 tablespoons raw honey

½ tablespoon orange essential oil

OTHER EQUIPMENT NEEDED

**Some kind of soap mold, like an old
wooden cheese box lined with
nonstick wax paper; you could
also use the bottom half of a milk
carton, a silicone cupcake pan, ice-
cube trays, or a shoe box.**

**Double boiler (I just put a glass bowl
over a pot of boiling water.)**

INSTRUCTIONS

Cube the soap base and add it to a double boiler. Stir constantly until the soap base is fully melted.

Allow the temperature to come back down slightly, until the soap thickens a bit. This prevents the add-ins from sinking to the bottom. Add the calendula and oatmeal. Stir until incorporated.

When the soap has cooled a little more, add in the honey and orange essential oil. I like to wait until the last minute, so they retain all of their raw properties.

Pour the melted soap into a mold. If you are using a wooden box, make sure to first line it with parchment paper. For soap that has a handmade look, use a spoon to make peaks in the top.

Before the soap completely hardens, sprinkle the top with a little more dried calendula.

Leave the soap mold in a spot where it can sit undisturbed until the soap hardens completely. This should take 3 to 4 hours.

Unmold the soap.

Slice into bars. You could get really precise here and measure to be sure each bar is even. I like to just go at it, throwing caution to the wind. It looks especially handmade with imperfections.

CHARCOAL TEA TREE SOAP

Activated charcoal is the detox darling of the natural beauty world. Its powerful drawing properties are said to pull toxins and bacteria from the skin.

INGREDIENTS

2 pounds melt-and-pour soap base (I use a goat's milk base, but shea butter is also a great option.)

4 teaspoons activated charcoal

1 teaspoon tea tree oil (also known as Melaleuca)

OTHER EQUIPMENT NEEDED

Soap mold

Double boiler (I just put a glass bowl over a pot of boiling water.)

INSTRUCTIONS

Cube the soap base and add it to a double boiler. Stir constantly until the soap base is fully melted.

Remove about a quarter cup of melted soap and add in the activated charcoal.

Incorporate the charcoal soap to the rest of the melted soap base.

When the soap has cooled a bit, add in the tea tree essential oil.

Pour the melted soap into a mold. For this soap, I use a square silicone mold.

Leave the soap mold in a spot where it can sit undisturbed until the soap hardens completely. This should take 3 to 4 hours.

Unmold the soap.

CHAMOMILE BODY BUTTER

A few simple ingredients come together to make this moisturizing cream that is safe enough for even the youngest members of the family. Historically, chamomile has been used for its anti-inflammatory properties. It has a faint apple scent and beautiful yellow color.

INGREDIENTS

½ cup coconut oil

½ cup olive oil

½ cup dried chamomile herb

½ cup shea butter

½ cup cocoa butter

INSTRUCTIONS

Make the infused oil by combining the coconut oil and olive oil in a double boiler, or a glass bowl over a pot of simmering water. Once the oils are melted, add in the dried chamomile. Allow the herbs to steep, like a tea, for about 30 minutes.

Using a fine mesh strainer, strain off the oil and discard the chamomile. (Feel free to skip the chamomile-infusing step and add in approximately 10 to 20 drops of chamomile or lavender essential oil.)

Add the shea butter and cocoa butter to the double boiler and stir until melted.

Pour everything into a glass jar with a lid. I like to store mine in two half-pint wide-mouth Mason jars.

The body butter should keep for a year, and yields approximately 16 ounces.

WHIPPED BODY BUTTER VARIATION

After the melting step, put the liquid in the freezer until it is firm. You don't want it to be completely solid, but just firm enough that when you push your finger into it, the imprint of your finger stays. Whip the butter using a stand mixer or handheld mixer. This results in a light and fluffy moisturizer. I gave this to my mom a few years ago, and every time she runs out, she asks me for more with a subtle, "Hey, umm, here's my empty body butter jar. Do you want it back?"

DIAPER CREAM

This little spin on the body butter recipe is perfect for healing diaper rash in no time flat. Usually I see improvement on the very first application. Bentonite clay has amazing healing benefits, as it absorbs moisture and removes toxins and impurities.

Add ½ cup shea butter and 4 tablespoons coconut oil to a double boiler. Once the mixture is melted, stir in 4 tablespoons each of zinc oxide and bentonite clay. Add in 5 drops lavender and/or Roman chamomile essential oil.

SUNSCREEN

To make the chamomile body butter, or the whipped body butter variation above, with a little SPF, add in ¼ cup of non-nano zinc oxide. Make sure to never use citrus essential oils in any body products that will be used prior to going in the sun as they are photosensitive, and can cause skin irritation and burning.

LAVENDER CALENDULA SALVE

Lavender essential oil and calendula are commonly used to speed up the healing process for a variety of skin injuries. They are soothing for rough skin, diaper rash, and minor cuts and burns. Since beeswax is excellent at sealing in moisture, it is a beautiful addition to this nourishing salve. All combined together, they are a dream for dry, itchy skin.

INGREDIENTS

¼ cup **coconut oil**

¼ cup **olive oil**

¼ cup **dried calendula**

¼ cup **shea butter**

½ cup **beeswax pellets**

20 drops lavender essential oil

INSTRUCTIONS

Make the infused oil by combining the coconut oil and olive oil in a double boiler, or a glass bowl over a pot of simmering water. Once the oils are melted, add in the dried calendula. Allow the herbs to steep, like a tea, for about 30 minutes. Using a fine mesh strainer, strain off the oil and discard the calendula.

Add the rest of the ingredients, except the lavender essential oil, to the double boiler and stir until melted.

Add in the lavender essential oil and stir until incorporated.

Pour everything into small candle tins, or a glass jar with a lid. I use five 2-ounce candle tins.

The salve should keep for a year, and yields approximately 10 ounces.

GRAPEFRUIT SUGAR SCRUB

I love sugar scrubs for their gentle ability to exfoliate dry and dead skin. The almond oil in this recipe is moisturizing, and the grapefruit lends a sweet, invigorating scent. Use at least once a week for soft and smooth skin. Follow with the Rose Lotion Bar from page 131 to lock in the moisture and leave skin extra silky.

INGREDIENTS

1 cup sugar
½ cup almond oil
10 to 20 drops grapefruit essential oil

INSTRUCTIONS

Add all of the ingredients to a Mason jar or crock and stir to combine.

LAVENDER CHAMOMILE BATH SALTS

There is nothing more satisfying than a piping hot bath after a long, cold winter day. I can lay there for hours with just my thoughts and the comforting warmth of the water. A little jar of bath salts next to the tub can transform an ordinary bathroom into a spa on even the busiest of days. The combination of oatmeal, Epsom salt, and sea salt is moisturizing, soothing, and detoxifying for the skin, while the herbs and essential oils promote relaxation.

INGREDIENTS AND MATERIALS

½ **cup oats**

½ **cup Epsom salt**

½ **cup sea salt**

¼ **cup dried lavender**

¼ **cup dried chamomile**

10 drops Roman chamomile essential oil

10 drops lavender essential oil

Muslin bags

INSTRUCTIONS

Combine the oats, salts, herbs, and essential oils in an airtight glass jar.

When you're ready to take a bath, fill a muslin bag until it is about two-thirds of the way full. Pull the drawstring closed.

Steep it in the bath like a tea bag.

Empty the herbs from the muslin bag and give it a good rinse. Lay it out to dry to use again for next time!

CITRUS BODY MIST

I'm sure it comes as no surprise that commercial perfumes are chock-full of synthetic fragrances that are better suited for outdoor areas with proper ventilation than up close and personal on your body. Essential oils, on the other hand, smell beautiful and have the added benefit of actually enhancing your health instead of detracting from it. Oils are so potent that they make the perfect addition to a fragrant homemade body mist.

INGREDIENTS

10 drops wild orange essential oil
5 drops lemon essential oil
5 drops lime essential oil
5 drops tangerine essential oil
¼ teaspoon real vanilla extract or 5 drops vanilla oleoresin
1 part witch hazel (or vodka)
2 parts water

INSTRUCTIONS

Add the essential oils and vanilla to a 2-ounce glass spray bottle. Fill it one-third of the way with witch hazel or vodka and top off with filtered water.

Shake before every use.

ORANGE TOOTHPASTE

Although teeth can be effectively polished with just a little baking soda, I like to keep a few extra ingredients on hand for taste, texture, and added tooth health benefits. Coconut oil is naturally antibacterial, and calcium carbonate provides minerals. I have read that orange essential oil aids in whitening, and it also provides a lovely orange taste that pairs well with the sweet xylitol. The up-front investment of making homemade natural toothpaste can be a little daunting, but after a year of making it yourself, and passing up the pricey natural brands at the store, you'll appreciate your efforts.

INGREDIENTS

2 tablespoons coconut oil, melted
2 tablespoons fractionated coconut oil*
3 tablespoons calcium carbonate
3 tablespoons xylitol
1 tablespoon baking soda
5 drops orange essential oil

* If you do not have fractionated coconut oil on hand, you can substitute it with regular coconut oil. I only add in the fractionated for the liquid consistency. Since coconut oil is solid at any temperature under 76 degrees, I find it easier to apply to the toothbrush when there is another liquid component. In the summer months, this isn't a concern at all.

INSTRUCTIONS

Mix all the ingredients in an airtight glass jar and store in a cool, dry place.

LEMON CLAY DEODORANT

If you're wrangling kiddos, pulling weeds in the garden, or creating an impressive from-scratch spread for the dinner table, you're probably working up a sweat on a daily basis. Simple living is hard work, no gym required. To avoid offending others with the natural by-product of your toil, try whipping up a batch or two of this homemade deodorant. Arrowroot powder is great for wicking away moisture, bentonite clay has natural detoxifying properties, and baking soda fights unpleasant smells. They are the odor-fighting trifecta. I add tea tree essential oil into my recipe for its antibacterial properties, and a few other oils for their pleasant scent.

INGREDIENTS

3 tablespoons coconut oil

1 tablespoon beeswax

1 tablespoon shea butter

4 drops lemon essential oil

4 drops lime essential oil

4 drops tea tree essential oil

4 drops cypress essential oil

1 tablespoon bentonite clay

4 tablespoons arrowroot powder

1 tablespoon baking soda

INSTRUCTIONS

Melt the coconut oil, beeswax, and shea butter in double boiler.

Remove the liquid from the heat and add in the essential oils.

Stir in the bentonite clay, arrowroot powder, and baking soda.

Pour the liquid into an empty deodorant container or a glass Mason jar.

Store in a cool, dry place for up to one year. This recipe makes enough to fill one standard deodorant container.

ORANGE CHAMOMILE LIP BALM

Yield: 20 tubes

This lip balm recipe is soothing and nourishing for dry lips. It comes together with a few basic ingredients that you probably already have in your stash if you are a DIY body goods maker like myself. Whip up twenty at a time and add one to each of the Christmas gifts you give this year!

INGREDIENTS

2 tablespoons coconut oil

2 tablespoons olive oil

2 tablespoons dried chamomile herb

2 tablespoons beeswax

2 tablespoons cocoa butter

10 drops orange essential oil

Lip balm tubes

INSTRUCTIONS

Combine the coconut oil and olive oil in a double boiler, or a glass bowl over a pot of simmering water. Once the oils are melted, add in the dried chamomile. Allow the herbs to steep, like a tea, for about 30 minutes. Using a fine mesh strainer, strain off the oil and discard the chamomile.

Add in the other lip balm ingredients.

Add the beeswax and cocoa butter to the double boiler. Heat the mixture over medium heat until they are melted together, stirring often.

Add the infused chamomile oil back to the double boiler, with the melted beeswax and cocoa butter.

Add the orange essential oil. Give it a stir.

Use a small funnel, or an old medicine dropper, to add the liquid lip balm mixture to the tubes. It will harden pretty quickly, so make sure to fill them right away.

Let sit for 10 minutes, or until cool and hardened.

ROSE LOTION BARS

For most of the year I don't really notice a need for lotion, but it's a different story when the dry air of winter rolls in. This lotion bar recipe is the perfect simple solution to soothe dry and itchy skin. Just rub it on and allow the oils to soak into dry skin. Shea butter and coconut oil are hydrating, while beeswax helps to hold the moisture in. Rose essential oil is known for its beneficial moisturizing and anti-aging properties. It also has the most soft and romantic scent. The oil is a bit pricey, so feel free to substitute lavender or geranium; the lotion will still have a bright floral scent. As always, you can just leave the essential oils out altogether if you prefer.

INGREDIENTS

½ cup beeswax
½ cup shea butter
½ cup coconut oil
10 to 20 drops rose essential oil
Silicone molds

INSTRUCTIONS

Heat the beeswax, shea butter, and coconut oil in a double boiler, until melted.

Remove the liquid from the heat and stir in the essential oil.

Pour the liquid into silicone molds and leave undisturbed until hardened.

Pop the lotion bars out of the molds, and enjoy!

EXFOLIATING CHARCOAL FACE SCRUB

I have to be honest—with a house, husband, and six kids to care for, most days feel like a marathon, with my cozy bed as the finish line. "My makeup has surely worn off by now anyway, right?" I tell myself as I jump straight under my crisp linen sheets.

A few years into my thirties, I started noticing wrinkles where I thought I had years of youthfulness left. After getting schooled by ladies who looked better than me in their forties, I decided to look into this whole skin-care routine business of regular face washing, exfoliation, and moisturizing. Exfoliation, which is to remove dry and dead skin cells, is an essential part of a regular skin-care routine. This simple exfoliating face scrub can help to improve circulation and detoxification.

INGREDIENTS

1 cup organic cane sugar
¼ cup almond oil
1 teaspoon activated charcoal
5 drops lavender essential oil

INSTRUCTIONS

Combine all the ingredients in a medium bowl and stir to combine.

Transfer the mixture to an airtight glass jar.

Gently work the mixture into your skin, and remove with warm water and a clean towel. Use once or twice a week for deep exfoliation and skin detoxification.

NATURAL WAYS TO CLEANSE

There are many natural ways to cleanse the skin, from using plain raw honey, a combination of oils and castile soap, or doing the ever-popular oil cleansing method. The key is to remove makeup and sweat from the day, without leaving your skin dry as a result of over-cleansing.

NATURAL WAYS TO MOISTURIZE

Some of the best natural oils for moisturizing skin are jojoba, olive, argan, and sweet almond. Consider making a salve or butter with some of these oils by combining them in a double boiler with beeswax or shea butter. You can also add in some healthy-skin essential oils, like frankincense, rose, or lavender. Take it up a notch by infusing one of the oils first with a little chamomile. Your skin will thank you.

CHAPTER 5

NATURAL CLEANING AND LAUNDRY

WHEN IT COMES TO CLEANING around the farmhouse, less is more. My approach is more of a "wipe and scrub as we go when something looks dirty." There are no harsh cleaners, so the kids can help do a lot of the work, too. Having survived eight-plus years now without all the conventional products, I can promise you, harsh chemicals aren't necessary to fight bacteria and shine the place up.

A few simple basic ingredients like vinegar, water, castile soap, and essential oils make up all-natural, yet effective, cleaning products for everything from counters and bathtubs to dishes and counters. I also like to keep a small stash of microfiber cloths and stainless-steel scrubbers for a little extra cleaning power.

We know a lot more these days about the harmful effects and air pollutants in conventional laundry detergents, but are there any great alternatives? Over the course of several years, and a lot of experimenting, I learned that there are inexpensive and natural ways to get laundry clean. With a few simple supplies, like citrus essential oils, castile soap, washing soda, and pieces of flannel and wool, we have eliminated the need for dryer sheets, store-bought detergents, and stain fighters. Laundry may not come out smelling like a tropical sunset, but clean, soft, and smelling "not bad" is good enough for me.

ALL-PURPOSE CLEANER

The lemon essential oil in this recipe is excellent at cutting grime and also provides a fresh scent. Tea tree oil (also known as Melaleuca) fights germs, bacteria, and viruses. Use this cleaner on any surface where an all-purpose cleaner is normally used.

INGREDIENTS

½ cup vinegar

1½ cups warm water

15 drops Melaleuca (tea tree oil)

15 drops lemon essential oil

INSTRUCTIONS

Combine everything in a glass spray bottle and give it a good shake.

Let the spray sit on the surface for 5 to 10 minutes, and then wipe away with a microfiber cloth or tea towel.

KITCHEN DISINFECTANT SPRAY

Sometimes I want something a little stronger for deep cleaning and disinfecting in the kitchen. A combination of alcohol, vinegar, and some powerful essential oils always does the trick. (**Note:** If you have stone countertops, check with the manufacturer to be sure that all the ingredients are safe to use on them.)

INGREDIENTS

1 cup water

½ cup distilled white vinegar

½ cup alcohol (rubbing alcohol or vodka)

20 drops tea tree essential oil

20 drops lemon essential oil (you can also use oregano, clove, eucalyptus, lavender, peppermint, lemongrass, cinnamon, rosemary, orange, or thyme essential oils)

GLASS CLEANER

Keeping glass clean in a home with six kids is mostly a losing battle. Nonetheless, it is handy to have glass cleaner on hand for bathroom mirrors, faucets, and the ever-so-rare desire to see through a crystal-clear window. It is easy to whip up, and requires the same basic supplies as most of the other homemade natural cleaners.

INGREDIENTS

2 cups water
¼ cup distilled white vinegar
10 drops lemon essential oil

INSTRUCTIONS

Combine everything in a glass spray bottle and give it a good shake. Apply it to glass surfaces, including mirrors and windows, and wipe away with a soft towel. The linen tea towels from page 7 or microfiber towels are both great choices for cleaning glass.

Shake well before each use to release that lemony fresh smell.

No lemon essential oil on hand? Add a few tablespoons of fresh lemon juice to a spray bottle. Top it off with water and start cleaning. This fresh preparation is best made on cleaning day and discarded afterward.

ORANGE DUSTING SPRAY

Most of the time a quick zip around the farmhouse with a microfiber cloth will take care of dust, but every once in a while I crave the scent and shine of a dusting spray. The olive oil in the recipe adds moisture and shine, while the vinegar provides the powerful cleaning and disinfecting action. Orange essential oil gives that lovely citrus scent you're used to with store-bought cleaners, but without any toxic chemicals. Most of the furniture in our house is white, but for those few natural wood pieces we have, a little spray goes a long way to buff out that lustrous sheen.

INGREDIENTS

1 cup water

½ cup distilled white vinegar

1 tablespoon olive oil

20 drops orange essential oil

INSTRUCTIONS

Combine all the ingredients in a glass spray bottle and shake to combine.

Shake well before each use, as the oil will rise to the top.

Make sure to label your glass spray bottles with a Sharpie, so you don't forget what is what between cleaning sessions. To print off some of the labels I use in my own home, visit farmhouseonboone.com/simple-farmhouse-life. To make my labels waterproof, I apply some clear packing tape over the top of them.

HARDWOOD FLOOR CLEANER

I often keep our hardwood floors clean with a microfiber cloth and a little water. More than anything else, we are sweeping dust bunnies and vacuuming the area rugs. The floors themselves usually just need spot cleaning. However, high-use areas, like the kitchen, need a little something extra once in a while. My beloved castile soap and citrus essential oils come to the rescue for a deep clean and fresh scent!

INGREDIENTS

⅛ cup castile soap

1 gallon warm water

10 drops orange essential oil

INSTRUCTIONS

Combine everything in a large bucket and clean the floors immediately.

TIPS FOR CLEANING HARDWOOD FLOORS

- Wring the wet mop or towel out before wiping the floor. Excess water on floorboards can damage and warp them over time, especially if they aren't sealed properly.

- Vacuum and sweep them often. When high-traffic areas are covered with dust and dirt, the surface will wear out over time. Use tools with soft bristles to avoid scratching and denting the wood.

- You only need a very small amount of soap to keep wood floors clean, especially if they are sealed properly.

SIMPLE LAUNDRY DETERGENT

With just a few basic ingredients on hand, this recipe can come together in a flash. If I go to the laundry cabinet and notice we are out of detergent, I can whip this one up faster than the washer can fill with water. The essential oil is optional, but it does add a subtle fresh scent. Some other great oil options for laundry detergent are lavender, geranium, lemon, and orange.

INGREDIENTS

2 5-ounce castile soap bars

2 cups washing soda

2 cups borax

20 to 30 drops orange essential oil (optional)

INSTRUCTIONS

Grate the castile soap bars with a cheese grater or food processor. Stir it together with the washing soda and borax. Add in the orange essential oil, if desired. For top-loading washers, use about ¼ cup of dry detergent per load. For a high-efficiency washing machine, 2 to 3 tablespoons should do the trick!

LIQUID LAUNDRY SOAP

For a liquid version of simple laundry detergent, add ½ gallon of hot water to a 5-gallon bucket and stir in the washing soda and borax. Grate the castile soap bars with a cheese grater or food processor. In a medium stockpot on the stove, dissolve the soap in a couple of cups of water, stirring constantly. Add the soap water to the borax and washing soda mixture. Add in the orange essential oil, if desired. Fill the 5-gallon bucket the rest of the way with warm water and give it a good stir.

After it sits overnight, the ingredients tend to separate a bit. Give it another vigorous stir, or use the paint-stir attachment on a drill to really incorporate everything and make it smooth. For top-loading washers, use about ½ to 1 cup of liquid detergent per load. For a high-efficiency washing machine, use about ¼ cup.

LAUNDRY SPOT REMOVER

Combine ⅔ cup water, ¼ cup liquid castile soap, and 10 drops of lemon essential oil in a spray bottle. Give the bottle a good shake and then spray the liquid directly on the stain. Unlike other stain treatments, this is not one that works better the longer it sits. It is best to get the load started pretty soon after applying the spot treatment.

LAVENDER DRYER SHEETS

If you are accustomed to adding dryer sheets to your laundry to get that "just washed" smell, the habit may be hard to kick when you make the switch to a more-natural laundry routine. It is simple to replace them, though, with vinegar, essential oils, and a quarter yard of flannel fabric. I like to store the extra vinegar mixture in the laundry room next to the dryer sheets. When one has gone through a load, I can just dip it in and add it back to the jar so it's ready to use the next time!

MATERIALS

Flannel fabric
1 cup distilled white vinegar
20 drops lavender essential oil

INSTRUCTIONS

Cut several 7-by-7-inch squares of flannel fabric.

Serge the edges, or create a hem around all four sides.

Add the vinegar and lavender essential oil to a Mason jar.

Dip each flannel square into the mixture and squeeze out the excess liquid.

Store the damp dryer sheets in an airtight glass container.

WOOL DRYER BALLS

Conventional dryer sheets are full of chemicals and fragrances that I don't want touching our skin. Handmade wool dryer balls are a simple and inexpensive way to reduce static cling, make clothes smell fresh, and cut down on drying time.

How do they work? Since wool is an absorbent fiber, the dryer balls pull in moisture from the wet clothes. The water is then slowly released back into the air during the drying process, causing more humidity. This reduces static cling. The balls bounce through the laundry, which softens the fabric and reduces dryer time.

Add five drops of essential oils to each dryer ball before starting the dryer and your laundry will come out smelling fresh, without the chemical cocktail of fragrance oils.

MATERIALS

One skein 100 percent wool yarn
One knee-high panty hose
Essential oils (optional)

INSTRUCTIONS

To start the wool ball, wrap a little yarn loosely around two of your fingers.

Once you've gone around ten to fifteen times, pull it off and wrap the yarn ten times around the center.

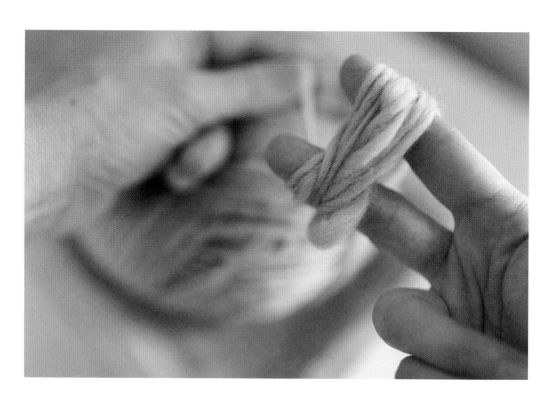

Continue wrapping, and changing directions, until you have a ball. Keep wrapping until you've used half the skein of yarn, and have a ball that is about the size of a tennis ball.

Cut the yarn and pull the end through the wool ball with a large needle or crochet hook.

Repeat with the rest of the yarn to make another dryer ball.

Put one ball down into a knee-high panty hose. Tie the hose in a knot and then put the other ball in. Tie another knot in the panty hose. Each ball should be in its own little section of panty hose.

Wash and dry the dryer balls with a few loads of laundry. It is best to wash them with loads that require hot water, like towels or linens. This will cause the wool to "felt," or press together.

Add two or three dryer balls to a load of laundry to shorten drying time and reduce static cling.

For a fresh scent, add several drops of essential oils to the dryer balls before throwing them in with each load of wet laundry.

Wool dryer balls should last for at least two years. A 120-yard skein of wool yarn will yield two dryer balls.

LAVENDER LINEN SPRAY

Linen spray is a great little addition to an all-natural laundry room. Use it to freshen up bedsheets, slipcovers, pillows, and clothes. Although *clean* doesn't really have a smell, it's nice to spread a bright floral scent around your home, without the use of unnatural scents and fragrance oils. Lavender essential oil is known for promoting relaxation and lowering anxiety levels, so this spray is especially beneficial to spritz on bed linens at nighttime.

INGREDIENTS

2 tablespoons witch hazel

20 drops lavender essential oil (you can also use lemon, orange, bergamot, geranium, patchouli, magnolia, or rose essential oils)

6 tablespoons water

INSTRUCTIONS

Using a funnel, add the witch hazel and lavender essential oil to a small glass spray bottle. Give it several shakes to combine the two.

Add the water.

Start spraying it everywhere that needs a little boost of freshness!

LAVENDER SACHETS

I have an old wooden chest in our bedroom that I purchased from the previous owners of our farmhouse. With its chipped black paint and aged wood interior, it is the perfect piece of furniture to house our extra sheets, quilts, and pillowcases. It has one lingering problem, though: It still smells faintly of mothballs, even after a thorough washing. These sachets are a great way to disguise the old smell with the calming scent of fresh lavender. Add them to sock drawers, blanket cupboards, or linen closets for an added boost of freshness.

MATERIALS

½ yard light- to medium-weight fabric, like linen, cotton, or a linen/cotton blend
1 cup uncooked rice
½ cup dried lavender
10 to 20 drops lavender essential oil

INSTRUCTIONS

Cut six squares of fabric, each measuring 5 by 5 inches.

With right sides together, sew two fabric squares together with a ¼-inch seam. Sew nearly all the way around, leaving a 1-inch opening. Clip the corners, being careful not to cut into your seam. Finish the seam with a serger or zigzag stitch, and turn the sewn square right side out.

Repeat for the other four squares of fabric so that you end up with three fabric squares.

In a medium bowl, combine the rice, dried lavender, and essential oils.

Use a funnel to pour the mixture into the fabric squares, dividing it evenly between the three.

Use a topstitch close to the edge to close the area that you left open for filling. Make sure to back- and forward-stitch to be sure you never have any rice or lavender spilling into your sock drawer.

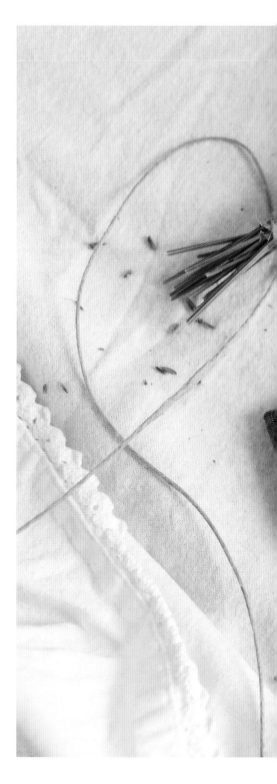

CHAPTER 6

HANDMADE GARDEN

I HAVE A FRIEND WHO LIVES IN THE CITY. Just outside her back patio door, she has utilized every square inch to grow the most beautiful variety of flowers. Every time I see her, she proudly presents me with a colorful arrangement in a reclaimed vase.

My view toward gardening used to be one of strict practicality. How else could I provide my family with organic zucchini, heirloom tomatoes, and all of the flavors of summer herbs? I'm not sure what it's like in your area, but we can find those things in abundance around here at the farmers' market or our local CSA.

My desire for a backyard garden is about the joy that comes from tilling the ground, planting a tiny seed, and watching the most beautiful intricate flower bloom in the hot summer sun. We love getting our hands dirty and teaching our children to understand where their food comes from. It's the same reason we care for our backyard chicken flock and load up the van every week to buy our milk from local farmers.

When we've been successful in coaxing something beautiful from the soil, we can bring the harvest inside to liven up the farmhouse with handmade wreaths and colorful dried bouquets. And when space and weather won't allow for outdoor growing, herbs and blooms can be grown indoors to enjoy summer's beauty year-round.

CONCRETE PLANTER

Concrete's color and texture lends itself well to my simple farmhouse style. My husband reminds me that he was crafting concrete planters long before they were cool. It's true—we have a planter on our porch the shape of a wicker wastebasket to prove it. Creating DIY concrete projects is also super easy and inexpensive.

MATERIALS

Cardboard

Packaging tape

Concrete powder

Water

Two mini bar clamps

Utility knife

INSTRUCTIONS

Make a mold by folding cardboard into the size you want and securing the sides with packaging tape. We made our large mold 13 inches long by 6 inches wide by 4 inches tall and our small mold, which fits inside the large mold, 11 inches long by 4 inches wide by 3 inches tall. This gave the concrete a thickness of 1 inch all the way around.

Mix concrete powder with water until it reaches a consistency a little thicker than pancake batter. (If the kind you're using has some large rocks in it, you can use a large plastic strainer to sift out most of it before adding water. This will produce a planter with a smoother finish.)

Cover the outside of the small mold, and the inside of the large mold, with packing tape. This gives it a nonstick surface. (At first we weren't sure how necessary this step was, but when we went to unmold the planter, the areas that hadn't been covered with tape did stick to the cardboard quite a bit. So this is definitely a necessary step!)

Fill the large mold about three-quarters of the way full. Press the small mold into the large mold. Add a weight to the small mold, to hold it down during the drying process. Top off the concrete so that the top of it is level with the top of the molds.

Use two clamps on opposite sides of the molds to hold them together. This prevents the cardboard from bowing.

Use something sharp, like a sharpened pencil or skewer, to poke through the inner mold and concrete to create drainage holes at the bottom of the planter.

Allow the concrete to sit undisturbed for about 24 hours. When it's dry, cut the cardboard molds away with a utility knife.

FORCING BULBS INDOORS

Try as I might to love all four seasons, wintertime gets me down every single year. Once the buzz of the holidays is over, the short days and rambunctious kids make me wish desperately for spring. I know winter has its merits—it's a time for rest and cozy blankets—but it just drags on a few months too long for my liking.

When March or April rolls around, those first few daffodils poking through the dirt remind me that long summer days are coming soon. My kids point out every budding tree, wildflower, and iris, yelling, "Sign of spring! Sign of spring!" We all get excited about the approaching warmer months.

Forcing bulbs indoors is a great way to enjoy the beauty of spring without having to wait endlessly for it. You are basically tricking bulbs into thinking it is time to make their seasonal debut, while you and I know the snow rages on outside.

Get creative with your potting vessel. I like to use antique pitchers, tureens, bowls, and cake stands. Baskets and whitewashed terra-cotta pots also make for a beautiful display.

MATERIALS

Vessel
Potting Soil
Bulbs

INSTRUCTIONS

Add draining rocks and potting soil to a potting container. Make sure the vessel you choose is at least 3 inches deep for root growth. Plant the bulbs, leaving about ½ inch of the top exposed.

Water the bulbs. Not too much, though; if the bulbs sit in standing water they will rot, so make sure to keep the soil moist, but not overly saturated.

Some bulbs, like paperwhites and amaryllis, can handle being potted straightaway. They are easy to force indoors, and perfect for beginners. Most others need a fifteen-week chilling period, between 35 and 45 degrees, before being grown indoors. You can do this in a refrigerator, unheated garage, shed, or even outside, in milder climates. (**Note:** If you choose to do this in a refrigerator, remember that ripening fruit gives off ethylene gas, which will damage the flowers inside the bulbs, so make sure to use an extra refrigerator, if you have one!)

Water the bulbs occasionally during the chilling process, as the soil becomes dry.

After the chilling period, bring the bulbs to a warm, dark location indoors. After a week or two, move them to a sunny location and watch them grow. Continue to keep the soil moist, but not overly saturated.

BEST BULBS TO FORCE INDOORS

Paperwhite	Daffodil	Crocus
Amaryllis	Tulip	Snowdrop
Hyacinth	Iris	Scilla

SIMPLE CUT-FLOWER GARDEN

There isn't much that can bring more life to this old farmhouse than a simple arrangement of fresh flowers harvested from our own cutting garden. Whether casually stuffed in an antique Mason jar or carefully arranged in a glass vase, they pretty much sum up summer's goodness.

I used to think it was frivolous to waste a few rows of precious garden space on something inedible. These days, I'm beginning to wonder if we should just scrap the edible portion altogether and stuff it to the hilt with zinnias and dahlias. Can't you just imagine hauling them in by the vintage basket full to make cheery little corners in every area of your home!

We still "waste" three-quarters of our garden space on herbs and veggies, but you can bet my cut-flower rows get a little extra water and hand-weeding attention.

The qualifications for excellent cut flowers are:
- They have long stems. You want something that can stand tall in a vase or Mason jar.
- They last at least five days after being cut. I love cutting flowers and creating arrangements, but I definitely don't have time to do it every day. Light blooms with strong stems do well for extended periods of time after they are cut.
- They're hardy to drought and weeds.
- For minimal effort and maximum blooms, select flower varieties that keep on producing like a tomato plant does—all summer long.

MY FAVORITE CUT-FLOWER VARIETIES

Zinnias

Cosmos

Dahlias

Sunflowers

Hydrangeas

Peonies

Wildflowers

TIPS FOR MAKING YOUR FLOWERS LAST LONGER

- Bring a bucket of water with you out to the garden. Usually it is no less than 80 or 90 degrees when I make it out to the garden to harvest summer flowers. I avoid having them wilt by immediately submerging them in water.

- Cut away any of the lower leaves and foliage that will be submerged underwater.

- Make a homemade flower preservative. Fill a quart Mason jar with warm water and add a couple of tablespoons each of sugar and vinegar. Give it a good shake.

- Change the water every other day, and when you do, trim the stems a bit.

BEAUTIFUL FLOWER ARRANGEMENTS

Creating a lively summer home with fresh blooms does take a little extra work each week, but it's something that even the kids can help with. I can't tell you how many hours my daughter Johanna has spent out in the garden clipping flowers and herbs and arranging them in Mason jars. Even my son proudly brings in his creations to place on the kitchen windowsill and bedside tables.

TIPS FOR CREATING SPECTACULAR FARMHOUSE-STYLE ARRANGEMENTS

- **Vary the vessel.** Think creatively with your flower vase choice. Large pitchers make bold statements as centerpieces if you have tall blooms. Tiny arrangements in vintage tin cups look lovely lined up on a windowsill. A tall skinny vase with one single bloom is understated elegance.

- **Include unopened blooms.** At first, the practice of cutting a flower before it reached full bloom just felt so wrong and wasteful to me. Once I realized how beautiful they looked—and also, how abundantly flowers can bloom if they're cut back often—I started purposely including several unopened flowers in my arrangements. I love the variety and visual interest that a newly formed zinnia bud, with its intricate scalloped layers, provides next to a bright cosmos that has lived out its full, happy life in the garden. The new and mature are all bunched together in a curated display of summer's bounty.

- **Add greenery.** Herbs from the summer garden add variety and freshness to casual farmhouse-style arrangements. The smell of freshly cut basil, wild chocolate mint, or overgrown cilantro pairs well with the barely there fragrance of zinnias. I like to let the herbs spill out over the sides, creating something both messy and beautiful.

- **Go for color!** I like to create a neutral backdrop in my home, so that the colors of each season can take center stage. Summer is the most colorful season in the farmhouse, with blooms in every shade of yellow, pink, blue, purple, and orange.

- **Arrange the larger flowers first.** It is easiest to begin flower arrangements by adding the largest flowers first. After they are spread out nicely throughout the vase, fill in with smaller blooms, adding greenery at the very end.

PRESSED FLOWER ART

When I choose to display something in my home, I like it to be my handpicked antiques, a favorite candid photo of the kids, or something natural from the garden. Pressed flower art is a great way to feature both a gorgeous antique frame and vibrant preserved color from spring and summer blooms.

MATERIALS

Flowers

Parchment paper

Heavy book for drying

Cardstock

Multipurpose glue

Antique frame

INSTRUCTIONS

Select and cut flowers.

If you are getting fresh-cut flowers from the garden or a hiking trail, make sure the morning dew has already dried, so that the flowers won't mold. (You can also use store-bought blooms or wildflowers, if need be.)

Since the colors will fade a bit during the drying process, select blooms that are the most vibrant. Green leaves, like ferns and ivy, look beautiful when added to the mix. Make sure the stems are short enough to fit inside whatever size frame you choose. I like to throw a few in without stems, as the blooms look pretty all on their own.

Arrange the flowers in a single layer on parchment paper and press inside the pages of a very heavy book. (If you still have an old phone book lying around, you can use that.) Stack a few other books on top for extra weight. Allow to sit for four weeks, or until the flowers completely dry. (If they are not fully dry, they may mold.)

Place your flowers on a piece of cardstock and move them around until you're satisfied with your arrangement. If your frame is smaller than a piece of standard cardstock, cut the sheet to size before you start arranging, so you know ahead of time what size area you'll be working with.

Once you know where you want to place your pressed flowers, brush a bit of multipurpose glue to the back of each one and lightly affix it to the cardstock. (You may need to water down the glue a touch first, if your flowers are extra delicate.)

I love to use antique frames for their unique character and patina, but you can use whatever you like. If your frame is much larger than a standard piece of cardstock, you can either use a larger photo mat, or cut a piece of posterboard to size.

BEST FLOWERS FOR PRESSED FLOWER ART

Although nearly any flower can be pressed, single-petal varieties like the following dry best:

Daisies	Zinnias
Queen Anne's lace	Cosmos
Pansies	Violas
Violets	Yarrow
Lavender	Larkspur
Poppies	Black-Eyed Susans

OTHER PRESSED FLOWER IDEAS

- Add pressed flowers to handmade cards for Christmas, birthdays, and showers. This is also a great way for kids to make something special for grandparents.

- Lightly glue pressed flowers to the inside of a glass Mason jar before pouring in wax to make candles.

- How pretty would it be to lightly press a couple of dried blooms into melt-and-pour goat's milk soap before it has hardened? These soaps make a beautiful addition to a handmade wedding gift basket.

HOW TO DRY FLOWERS

At the end of summer when the temps start to dwindle at night and you see that first frost in the forecast, head out to the garden and get an armful, or two, of those fresh garden flowers. With minimal effort and a little time, you can preserve their beauty to enjoy for the rest of the year.

INSTRUCTIONS

Cut the flowers after the morning dew has dried, but before the heat of the day sets in.

Remove excess leaves from the flower stems.

Create small bundles with the flowers, and secure them at the stems with string.

Hang them in a dry, well-ventilated area, on a line or hooks. To make sure the flowers retain their color, choose an area that is also dark. To ensure proper air circulation, don't overcrowd the blooms.

Allow them to dry for about two weeks, or until fully dry.

TIPS FOR DISPLAYING DRIED FLOWERS

- Add them to vases and pitchers for tabletop and windowsill displays.

- Hang bundles of flowers on hooks in the kitchen to enjoy their beauty all winter long.

- Arrange them into a colorful front-door wreath, like the one found on page 179.

MAKING A WREATH

While wreaths are beautiful on the front door, they also have the potential to add beauty and life to every room in the home. I like to use whatever is seasonally available to reflect the changing colors outside and capture a little of that beauty to bring indoors. They look pretty hung with a little ribbon from windowsills, on cupboard doors, and draped over large vintage mirrors.

Dried florals and preserved greenery are great for wreath making because they can be kept year after year, but sometimes it doesn't hurt to make a wreath with the fresh stuff. Sure, it won't endure throughout the seasons, but you can appreciate its beauty while it's up, and they only take a few minutes to make!

MATERIALS

Grapevine or wire wreath form
Floral wire
Any combination of dried flowers, greenery, eucalyptus, preserved boxwood, dried herbs, faux florals, twigs, or pinecones
Hot glue
Ribbon or fabric scraps (optional)

INSTRUCTIONS

If you are using a grapevine wreath form, tuck the ends of whatever stem you are working with into the wreath form. Secure them with floral wire wrapped around the base. For a wire wreath form, first secure the ends of the stems into little bundles with floral wire. Secure the bundles to the form with more floral wire. If you are using something that does not have a long stem, you can use a little hot glue to secure it to the wreath form. This is a great way to fill in gaps in the wreath with blooms that have fallen off the stems.

Continue to work little by little, and adjust the stems to make it have the same fullness all the way around. I like to use a variety of different greens and /or florals, depending on the season, and just mix them all in evenly.

Tie a large fabric scrap, or ribbon, into a bow. Slip a piece of floral wire through the tie, and secure around the back of the wreath form. I love to use ticking-stripe fabric, linen, or burlap to add an extra pretty detail to my wreaths.

You can either slip your wreath straight onto a metal wreath hanger, or secure it to a nail with a little floral wire in the back. Another hanging option is to add a little ribbon through the top of the wreath and tack it to the back of a cabinet or hutch door.

IDEAS FOR WREATHS YEAR-ROUND

- In the springtime, go out and gather greenery and branches from blooming trees. Tuck them loosely into a grapevine wreath form and enjoy them like you would a bouquet of fresh flowers.

- Cut branches and pinecones from any evergreen trees you have nearby. Create small bundles with floral wire and attach them to a wire wreath form. Stuff a few pieces of fresh eucalyptus throughout the wreath to mix up the colors. Attach pinecones and berries with hot glue or wire, and add a red ribbon for a little extra seasonal color.

- Enjoy a faux lavender wreath year-round. Create small bundles with floral wire and attach them to a grapevine or wire wreath form. Add a large fabric bow to the top and hang it over the door on a decorative wreath hanger.

DRIED-FLOWER WREATH

I love to decorate our farmhouse with natural elements, and drying flowers is a great way to enjoy the colors throughout the seasons. The bright summer florals fade to pretty pastels that brighten up any room in the house. They look lovely stuffed in a pitcher in the dining room, or arranged into a colorful wreath. Dry out sunflowers for a fall front-porch wreath, or hydrangeas for a beautifully full wreath. I like to mix and match and create a look that is a bit wild and messy.

MATERIALS

Several bundles of dried flowers

Floral wire

Wreath form (Grapevine or wire forms both work great!)

Hot glue (optional)

Jute string

INSTRUCTIONS

Trim the flowers so that the stems are about 4 to 6 inches long.

Create small bundles and secure them at the base of the flowers with floral wire.

Work around the wreath form, attaching the small bundles with floral wire in a circular fashion. Tuck the stems behind the wreath form and secure with more floral wire.

Use hot glue to attach large flower heads in sparse spaces that need to be filled in.

Trim any excess stems and floral wire.

Tie a jute string to the back of the wreath form to hang on a wreath hanger or nail.

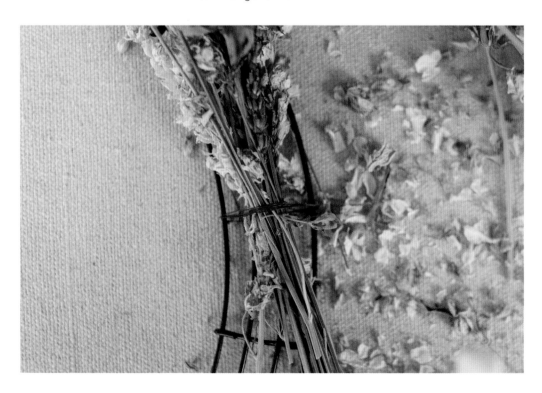

FRESH HERB WREATHS

These little wreaths are only really practical during the hot summer months, when your garden is overflowing with more herbs than you know what to do with, or you can buy them in abundance at the farmers' market. Instead of throwing them straight into the refrigerator, wrap them into a simple wreath to enjoy their beauty while grabbing a pinch of rosemary for your stew or a touch of thyme for your chicken. During especially bountiful garden months, I like to enjoy these wreaths just for the beauty of the herbs hanging in my kitchen, without picking at them to use in dishes.

MATERIALS

Fresh herbs

Small wreath form

Floral wire

Ribbon or jute twine for hanging

INSTRUCTIONS

If you plan to eat the herbs from the wreaths, wash them with cold water and lay them out to dry on a tea towel. Make sure the herbs are completely dried out to avoid mold.

Create small bundles of herbs and wrap them at the base with floral wire.

Secure each bundle of herbs to the wreath form with floral wire. Overlap the bundles slightly, so the herbs from one covers up the wire-wrapped base from the previous one. Continue adding bundles of herbs until the entire wreath form is covered.

Use kitchen hooks (or a small nail) and a piece of jute twine to display the wreaths in the kitchen. They last longer in a dark place, and will naturally dry out as they hang.

BEST HERBS FOR WREATH MAKING

Any herbs that you have growing in abundance are great choices for these quick wreaths, like that overgrown chocolate mint patch or the lemon balm threatening to take over the garden, but some herbs definitely hold their shape longer than others. Try rosemary, sage, thyme, or a combination of all three for longer-lasting fresh kitchen decor.

WINDOWSILL HERB GARDEN

I love the bright flavor of homegrown herbs in meats, soups, eggs, and veggies. Although nothing can match the abundance of a summer herb garden, it is still possible to get a little dash of that fresh taste in your home year-round by growing a windowsill herb garden.

MATERIALS

Organic seed starting mix or potting soil

Planters with adequate drainage

Seeds, seedlings, or plants

A south-facing window and/or LED plant-growing lights

Tray or plate to catch excess water

INSTRUCTIONS

Add an organic potting soil to a planter with proper drainage.

Plant a seed, seedling, or mature plant.

Add fresh water.

Place the pot on a south-facing windowsill, atop a tray or plate to catch excess water.

Repeat until you have potted all the herbs your heart desires!

TIPS FOR GROWING HERBS INDOORS

- Provide adequate light. Most herbs need 6 hours of direct sunlight every single day. The best option for a windowsill herb garden is a south-facing window.

- If you don't have a window in your home that provides enough light, you can still successfully grow indoor herbs with LED plant-grow lights. If you notice that your herbs aren't thriving, it may be necessary to supplement the natural light.

- Check the moisture level often. When the soil is dry to the touch, offer your plants a little water. Some plants need more than others, so continual observation is the best policy.

- Re-pot plants if they seem to be outgrowing their current home.

- Keep them in a warm place, ideally between 65 and 70 degrees.

- Use lukewarm water for watering.

- Choose a potting mix that is designed for optimal drainage.

CLAY HERB MARKERS

These simple herb markers come together with just a few basic supplies and very little hands-on time. They look pretty next to bright green herbs in a terra-cotta pot. Use them in planters to freshen up the house for spring, or in those pots that contain easy-to-grow windowsill herbs, to enjoy a little life year-round.

MATERIALS

Air-dry clay

Rolling pin

Ruler

Pen

Knife

Parchment paper

Oil-based paint marker

INSTRUCTIONS

Roll the air-dry clay out with a rolling pin until it is about ¼-inch thick.

Use a straight edge and pen to etch a rectangle that is 4½ inches long by 1 inch wide, into the clay. At the top of the rectangle use two ½-inch slanted lines to create a point. Continue etching until you have the number of plant markers that you want to create.

Use a knife to cut out all the plant markers.

Carefully transfer the cutouts to a piece of parchment paper and allow them to sit out until they are completely dry.

Use an oil-based paint marker to write the name of each herb you are going to pot on the clay cutouts.

DRYING HERBS

Herbs are among the easiest plants to grow. Although abundant all summer long, that first frost sends many varieties into a sad brown pile on your garden floor. To capture the summer bounty, and to season your winter stews, drying is the best method of preservation. For optimal flavor, it is best to harvest the herbs somewhere in the middle of the season, before they have gone to seed.

AIR-DRY METHOD

This works best for low-moisture herbs, like thyme, sage, rosemary, and oregano.
- Cut the herbs after the morning dew has dried, but before the heat of the day sets in.
- Remove wilted leaves and bugs.
- Create small bundles with the herbs and secure them at the stems with string.
- Hang them in a dry, well-ventilated area, on a line or hooks.
- Allow them to dry for ten days.

OVEN METHOD

This works best for high-moisture herbs like basil, parsley, and mint.
- Cut the herbs after the morning dew has dried, but before the heat of the day sets in.
- Remove wilted leaves and bugs.
- Spread out the herbs on a cookie sheet.
- Turn your oven on as low as it will go, ideally no higher than 170 degrees, and then turn it off. Allow the herbs to dry in the warm oven for about an hour. At this point the herbs may be dry, or they may need you to turn the oven back on for a bit, to reach about 120 degrees. Some herbs will dry more quickly than others.
- You will know your herbs are completely dry when they crumble between your fingers. Store the dried herbs in an airtight container in a dark place for up to one year.

SCRAP-FABRIC PLANT HANGER

Finished plant hanger length: 36 inches

The charm of this simple decor piece is in its imperfections. Made from humble fabric scraps, it proves that beauty can be found in something destined for the trash can. For my plant hanger, I used leftover bleached drop cloth from one of my slipcovering projects. Next to the fresh green color of a potted mint plant, I think the loose strings and unfinished fabric look lovely in our old farmhouse.

MATERIALS

Several strips of scrap fabric (Linen, canvas, cotton, and duck are all great options; avoid stretchy knit fabrics.)

Small to medium potted indoor plant

MEASURE AND CUT

Three 52-inch-by-¾-inch strips

Three 38-inch-by-¾-inch strips

INSTRUCTIONS

Join the three 52-inch pieces with one large knot 3 inches from the top. Once the knot is tied, the top of the knot should fall right at 2 inches from the top.

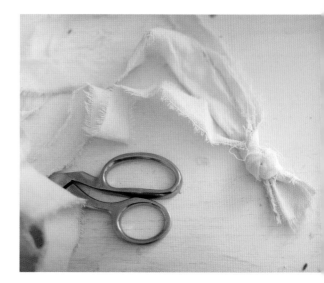

From the bottom of the large knot, go down one of the long pieces 10½ inches and tie one of the short (38-inch) strips in place, leaving a 2½-inch tail, from the 38-inch piece, coming out of the top of the knot.

At this point the bottom of the short piece should line up with the bottom of the long piece that it is attached to.

Repeat to join the other two short strips to the other two long strips. Make sure all three middle knots line up with each other.

Next, go down from one of the three middle knots 5 inches. You will have two fabric strips coming from each knot. Join a strip coming from one of the middle knots to a strip coming from the next knot over. Repeat in a circular fashion until all three sections are connected with three knots. All three knots should line up.

Go down another 5 inches and make another circular row of knots.

Lastly, go down a final 5 inches and make one giant knot with all six pieces.

Trim the strips to make them all even, if necessary.

FRONT-PORCH PLANTERS

During our first summer in our Victorian farmhouse, we discovered that the previous owners had left behind several vintage stoneware crocks, ranging from a couple of bulky 10- and 12-gallon containers down to some more-modest 3-gallon ones. You can bet I had my heart set on arranging them all beautifully on the porch with herbs and flowers, which is just what I did.

If I'm really ambitious in the fall, I stuff them with mums next to an heirloom pumpkin collection. Our antique home even has a small side porch that can handle a terra-cotta pot of herbs and zinnias, or a fern or two. One of the quaint little cottages on the property came equipped with window boxes that are just perfect for a colorful cottage flower mix.

If you're lucky enough to have a house with a front porch, rocking chairs, and a porch swing, you'd better take full advantage with a few front-porch planters. Even if your porch is small, you can still enjoy the colors of summer on a hot day with fresh potted herbs, flowers, and greenery. I like to create front-porch planters in late spring when the danger of frost has passed, to enjoy their beauty all summer long.

TIPS FOR CREATING BEAUTIFUL FRONT-PORCH PLANT ARRANGEMENTS

- **Use creative planters.** Keep your eye out for vintage crocks, butter churns, galvanized washtubs, and wooden crates at antique and thrift shops. Classic terra-cotta pots in various heights are also stunning.

- **Vary the plant heights.** If your planters are similar in size, try placing one on an antique chair or stool to elevate it above the others. I like to put a planter on either side of the door, or create groups of three. They also look great going up front-porch steps, if you have them.

- **Add in some herbs and greens.** I love the added green that a couple of kale, basil, or mint plants add to a potted arrangement. Plus, if you're in a pinch for a fun summer lemonade garnish, look no further than the front porch.

- **Choose some plants that will spill over the outside of the pot,** like creeping Jenny, English ivy, or green coleus.

- **Try adding large planters to other areas besides the porch.** Vintage washtubs look especially pretty sitting on mulch next to the other plants and trees in front-yard landscaping.

Planters

Potting soil

Plants

Holes in the bottom of the pot are ideal for drainage, but if you are using something that isn't appropriate for drilling, you can add rocks to the bottom. This method is great, but if you over-water, you still risk the roots rotting out. Since summer doesn't last forever, this method is likely A-okay as long as you're careful with watering. (**Hint:** Maybe don't give your three-year-old the watering job if you use this drainage method.) Another way to add drainage is to put all the plants into a pot that will fit inside your planter. Elevate the pot on an upside-down bowl in the bottom of the planter.

Fill the planter with soil. Leave a few inches from the top to have space to add the plants. I like to use an organic potting soil that is made for container gardening because it provides better drainage than topsoil or fill dirt.

Of course, you could plant from seeds, but I like to use plants from the nursery so I can mix and match the colors and heights of the plants. Before removing the plants and disrupting their roots, play around with the arrangement options on the ground. Once you are happy with the way the plants look together, create a small hole in the potting soil, add the plant, and pat down gently around it. Add the rest of the plants.

Water as necessary when the top inch or two of soil is dry. In the middle of summer, if you live in a warm climate, you will probably have to water daily. Here in the Midwest, we get some serious scorchers in July and August, so the topsoil dries out pretty quickly.

PLANTS FOR FRONT-PORCH PLANTERS

Zinnias	Thyme	Geraniums
Rosemary	Marigolds	Petunias
Hydrangeas	Daisies	Basil
Violas	Ferns	Lavender
Lobelias	Pansies	Impatiens
Ivy	Mint	Coleus

CEDAR RAISED GARDEN BEDS

Finished dimensions: 6 feet long by 3 feet wide

One of the first projects we tackled when we moved to our seven acres was cedar raised garden beds. Every year we till up a modest plot to grow a few rows of tomatoes, zucchini, herbs, and fresh-cut flowers, and the raised beds help us to be more organized about it. We placed the cedar beds in front of a sweet little building that sits just south of our old white barn, and we now call it our garden cottage. Raised garden beds allow you to grow a lot of food in a small space, and the beds are much easier to weed because they are raised off the ground.

MATERIALS

Six 6-foot pieces of cedar (we use 6-foot long cedar fence posts)

Six 10-inch-long 1x2s, or 2x4s ripped in half

Screws

Circular saw

Drill

INSTRUCTIONS

If you're using cedar fence posts, cut off the top of the post. This isn't something you have to do. We square off the top to make it look a little cleaner.

Measure the cedar fence posts. Cut two boards in half. Each of our posts was 6 feet long, so we cut each in half to make two 3-foot boards. These will be the ends of each raised bed.

Take two of the long pieces of cedar, lay them next to each other, and line up the ends.

Place one of the 10-inch-long 2x4s cut in half (or 1x2s) to one of the ends of the long cedar boards and drill in.

Stand it up so that the cedar board is touching the table, the ripped 2x4 is up, and part of it is above the cedar.

Place the short end piece next to the long piece, creating a 90-degree angle, and screw it into the ripped 2x4. Continue doing this until all four boards are attached.

Add the second layer of cedar posts and screw them into the ripped 2x4s. In the center of the long side of the raised bed, screw in another ripped 2x4. This helps add support so it doesn't bow out once the soil is added.

Put the finished beds in place and add soil. When installing raised beds, it is a good idea to allow enough space between each bed to make it comfortable to walk through and bend down.

WHY CEDAR?

Cedar is a naturally rot-resistant lumber. Also rot-resistant and long-lasting is redwood, but it is very expensive. Douglas fir is an affordable option, but it won't last as long as redwood or cedar. Pressure-treated wood leaches chemicals (such as fungicides and copper) into the soil and is not approved for organic use.

I AM BEGINNING TO LEARN THAT
IT IS THE SWEET, SIMPLE THINGS
OF LIFE WHICH ARE THE REAL
ONES AFTER ALL.
—LAURA INGALLS WILDER

I'VE READ EVERY SINGLE Laura Ingalls Wilder book to my kids multiple times, and now Luke is working through the series with them as I type away at this book. Nothing about their lifestyle back in the early nineteenth century was easy. Just when Pa Ingalls thought they would finally have a big-enough grain crop that they wouldn't have to worry about their next meal, the grasshoppers came in and destroyed it. It is hard for us to fathom, with our comfy modern houses and well-stocked grocery stores, the desperation they felt when a particularly long winter nearly took their lives.

I wouldn't trade living in this modern era for anything. It is a special time in history when we can enjoy the process of knitting a blanket with our two hands without having to first shear a sheep and spin the yarn on a wheel. We can learn to bake ancient sourdough bread and create heirloom starters with grain that we put through an electric grain mill. If you were too busy writing a book to get your seeds started early (wink, wink), a quick trip to the nursery will catch you right up with all the other gardeners enjoying those Fourth of July tomatoes.

Every once in a while I get messages and e-mails from people who point out my six kids, home-based business, and farmhouse restoration and criticize my simple lifestyle as being anything but. "If you had no kids, an apartment, and a regular job, you'd truly understand simple living," they've told me.

I think the confusion people have is between simple and easy. Raising kids and restoring a farmhouse we love is hard, but we get the unique joy of watching our hard work blossom into something beautiful. There is satisfaction in connecting with our handmade past and learning old-fashioned skills that were passed down for generations. Instead of rushing from one activity to the other, we are intentional about long days at home as a family, making three meals in the kitchen, getting our hands dirty in the garden, and learning how to create basic items from raw materials.

Sewing linen dresses, whipping up a fluffy batch of body butter, and baking bread from scratch isn't practical or necessary. Just go online or to a farmers' market and you can find artisans who will gladly sell you all three. The first time you sew something for your little girl, the seam will be crooked and the sleeves slightly uneven. You will spend more money and time making that dress than if you had just bought it, but I promise you, you'll never treasure a clothing item so much. As you learn to create things around your home, your skills will improve and you will start to think of many more beautiful ways to customize and personalize them.

Back in the pioneer days, Laura felt so much joy in quiet days spent at home, washing dishes, crocheting fine lace edges on towels, and listening to Pa play his fiddle. Simple, handmade living is a worthwhile pursuit that we modern folks can get a taste of, no matter where we live or what season of life we're in.

Antiques: I like to browse my local antiques shops, but when I want something specific, I use Etsy.com.

Beeswax: Beesworks beeswax pellets on Amazon.com

Double-gauze fabric: GauzeFabricStore.com

Drop cloth: Chicagocanvas.com

Grain-sack fabric: PrimitivesbyKathy.com (search "fabric")

Linen fabric: I love Robert Kaufman linen-blend fabric on Amazon.com and fabric.com.

Sewing tutorials: For my free sewing course, visit FarmhouseonBoone.com/Simple-Sewing -Series. I share video tutorials on all the basics, from the supplies you'll need to get started, to creating a hem, seam, or ruffle—and so much more!

ABOUT THE AUTHOR

Lisa Bass is the author and photographer behind the Farmhouse on Boone website. She began the blog in December of 2015 to share from-scratch recipes, natural living, and her simple handmade home. In May of 2018, her husband, Luke, quit his job to come home and help with the business full-time. They are currently restoring a nineteenth-century Victorian farmhouse and a seven-acre plot of land, complete with an old barn and silo. They are busy each day taking care of their six kids, knocking out one project at a time, and sharing it all with the world through their blog and YouTube channel.